Designing Menus with Encore DVD

John Skidgel

CMP**Books**

San Francisco, CA • New York, NY • Lawrence, KS

Published by CMP Books
an imprint of CMP Media LLC
Main office: 600 Harrison Street, San Francisco, CA 94107 USA
Tel: 415-947-6615; Fax: 415-947-6015

Editorial office:
4601 West 6th Street, Suite B, Lawrence, KS 66049 USA
www.cmpbooks.com
email: books@cmp.com

Designations used by companies to distinguish their products are often claimed as trademarks. In all instances where CMP is aware of a trademark claim, the product name appears in initial capital letters, in all capital letters, or in accordance with the vendor's capitalization preference. Readers should contact the appropriate companies for more complete information on trademarks and trademark registrations. All trademarks and registered trademarks in this book are the property of their respective holders.

The programs in this book are presented for instructional value. The programs have been carefully tested, but are not guaranteed for any particular purpose. The publisher does not offer any warranties and does not guarantee the accuracy, adequacy, or completeness of any information herein and is not responsible for any errors or omissions. The publisher assumes no liability for damages resulting from the use of the information in this book or for any infringement of the intellectual property rights of third parties that would result from the use of this information.

Senior Editor:	Dorothy Cox
Editor:	Rita Sooby
Production Editor:	Gail Saari
Technical Editor:	Richard Young
Layout Design:	John Skidgel
Cover Layout Design:	John Skidgel and Damien Castaneda

Distributed in the U.S. by:
Publishers Group West
1700 Fourth Street
Berkeley, CA 94710
1-800-788-3123

Distributed in Canada by:
Jaguar Book Group
100 Armstrong Avenue
Georgetown, Ontario M6K 3E7 Canada
905-877-4483

For individual orders and for information on special discounts for quantity orders, please contact:
CMP Books Distribution Center, 6600 Silacci Way, Gilroy, CA 95020
Tel: 1-800-500-6875 or 408-848-3854; fax: 408-848-5784
email: cmp@rushorder.com; Web: www.cmpbooks.com

ISBN: 1-57820-235-3

Dedication

For their unwavering support and love, I dedicate this book to my parents, Herbert and Blanca Skidgel, and to my wife, Allison.

Contents

Acknowledgements

Thanks to Dorothy Cox, Damien Castaneda, Gail Saari, Rita Sooby, and Paul Temme at CMP Books, for helping me realize this book. Cheers to the Encore DVD team, my colleagues, for creating a great product. Gratitude to Bill Bachman and Dave Trescot for supporting this book. Much appreciation to Richard Young, my technical editor, for pushing for more explanations. The last round goes to Joel Gardner and James Park, my video production cohorts, for assisting with the video shoots.

Introduction

Developing a DVD requires several stages: acquisition, editing, menu design, linking, compression, quality assurance, usability testing, and replication. This book is about menu design with Adobe Encore DVD. You will learn how to create functional, aesthetically pleasing menus.

Menu design is a crucial part of the DVD authoring process because menus are the interface between viewers and the content stored on the DVD.

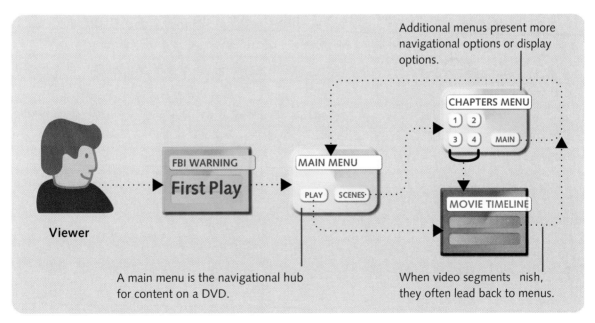

Figure 1-1: Relationship between the viewer and menus on a DVD

How this Book is Organized

To help you design better menus, this book explains all the facets of DVD menu design. The book is organized into four sections: Introduction, Designing for the Screen, Creating Still Menus, and Creating Motion Menus. A set of appendices, a glossary, and an index round out the book's offering.

Section One: Introduction

You're reading Chapter One, which gives you an overview of the book, tips on how to use the book, and hardware and software prerequisites.

Chapter Two discusses the DVD specification as it relates to menus. It covers the structure of a menu and the differences between still and motion menus, NTSC and PAL video formats, and normal and wide screen aspect ratios. I include a descriptive list of the different types of menus you can create for projects at the end of the chapter.

Section Two: Designing for the Screen

Chapter Three explains interaction design for DVD menus. It includes strategies for gathering requirements, mapping interactions, and testing prototypes. If you're new to interface design, you'll want to read this chapter. Chapter Four covers graphic design for DVD menus. This chapter is a primer for visual design topics such as layout, color, typography, imagery, and animation.

Section Three: Creating Still Menus

Chapter Five gives you an insider's tour of the Encore DVD interface, paying particular attention to menu design and editing functions. Chapter Six gives tips for preparing images for menus. Chapter Seven is a collection of tutorials that guide you through the process of creating still menus in Encore DVD and Photoshop.

Section Four: Creating Motion Menus

Chapter Eight distinguishes between the different types of motion menus. You'll learn how still imagery or motion combine with sound to create different kinds of menus. You will also learn how to create introductory and transitional animations. At the end of Chapter Nine, you will create a chapter selection menu with video thumbnails for each button.

Chapter Ten shows you how to create motion menus with Adobe After Effects. It begins with an overview of the interface, and three motion menu tutorials follow.

Icon Glossary

Important information is separated from the main body of text by a light gray background, and several types of callouts (Figure 1-2) list the kinds of notes you will find throughout the book.

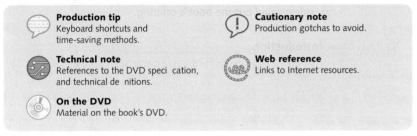

Production tip
Keyboard shortcuts and time-saving methods.

Cautionary note
Production gotchas to avoid.

Technical note
References to the DVD speci cation, and technical de nitions.

Web reference
Links to Internet resources.

On the DVD
Material on the book's DVD.

Figure 1-2: **Icon glossary**

How to Use the Book and DVD

If you're new to digital video, design, and DVD authoring, read the entire book. It will give you a good foundation in this exciting new medium. If you are an experienced video editor or motion graphics designer, you should read Chapters Two and Chapters Six through Nine. If you have DVD authoring experience but are new to Encore DVD, Photoshop, or After Effects, read Chapters Five through Nine.

The DVD has a lot of resources on it, including templates for planning your project as well as assets for all the tutorials. The DVD also will play in a set-top player and show samples of the menus available on the DVD.

If you are looking for more reference material, book updates, and related information, go to http://www.skidgel.com/encorebook/index.html.

Before You Begin

Adobe Encore DVD has several hardware and software requirements. The following pages list these requirements and offer additional advice in configuring your computer for DVD authoring.

Required Software

Adobe Encore DVD is a lot like a page layout application because it is the last leg of a publishing system. You create assets in other applications and then import them into Encore DVD to "publish" a DVD. Adobe Photoshop, After Effects, and Premiere Pro have tight integration with Encore DVD, and this book covers how to make the most of Encore DVD with these applications. Figure Figure 1-3 shows the interaction between the applications.

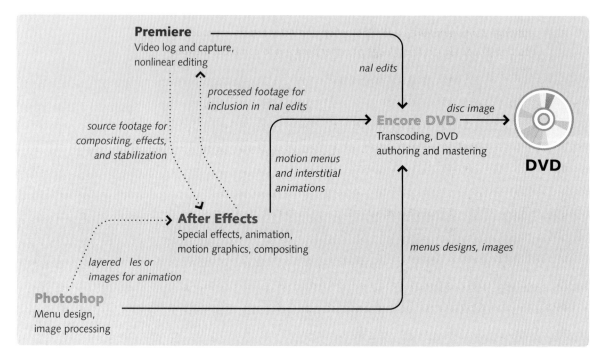

Figure 1-3: **Applications used in DVD menu design**

OPERATING SYSTEM

Encore DVD requires either Windows XP Professional or Windows XP Home Edition to run. Encore DVD will not run on Windows NT, 2000, or 98.

ADOBE PHOTOSHOP

Section Two explains how to use Encore DVD with Photoshop; you will frequently switch between the two applications. If you plan to edit your menus outside of Encore DVD or would like to use the Edit in Photoshop feature, you will need Photoshop. Photoshop 7 is referenced in this book.

ADOBE AFTER EFFECTS

Section Three covers how to create motion menus with Adobe After Effects. If you want to go beyond the simple chapter index-style motion menu, you will need After Effects.

 Although some familiarity with Photoshop and After Effects is expected, you don't need expert knowledge of either program to complete the tutorials.

Suggested Software

You do not need the following applications to run Encore DVD, but they are incredibly helpful in producing a DVD. These are my recommendations, but feel free to use whatever you are most comfortable with.

NONLINEAR EDITOR

You use a nonlinear editor (NLE) to capture, edit, and output video for use in Encore DVD. If you do not currently own a video editor, get Premiere Pro because it has superb integration with Encore DVD. For example, chapter markers can be embedded in MPEG-2 video files exported from Premiere and used in Encore DVD. It also has many powerful features such as real-time video and audio editing. I used Premiere Pro to capture and edit all the video content for this book.

A DRAWING OR DIAGRAMMING TOOL

Either Microsoft Visio or Adobe Illustrator are great tools for creating planning diagrams, referred to as "flowcharts," of complex DVD projects. Use Visio if you want something that does not require a lot of computer drawing skills. Use Illustrator if you want the ability to customize your diagrams or want to integrate Photoshop files. Both files also can be used to create wireframes for complex and highly interactive DVD projects.

SPREADSHEET OR PROJECT TRACKING SOFTWARE

If you are managing DVD production, consider an application that helps with planning schedules. Microsoft Excel, Project, or Visio can be used for these tasks.

Required Hardware

Figure Figure 1-4 shows a typical hardware configuration for DVD menu design.

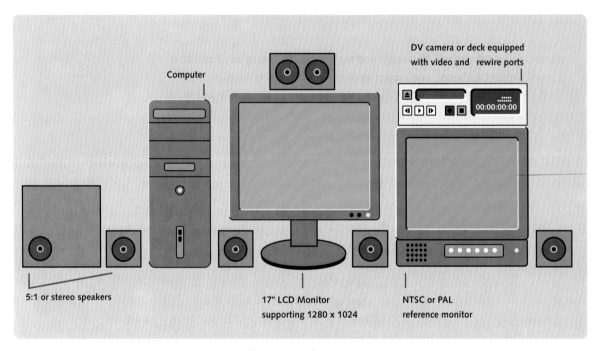

Figure 1-4: **A typical computer configuration**

COMPUTER AND PROCESSOR

An Intel® Pentium® III 800MHz processor is the minimum requirement. I suggest purchasing the fastest Pentium processor you can afford and consider purchasing a system with Intel's hyper threading technology or a multiprocessor system. Menu rendering, MPEG-2 video encoding, and disc burning all run faster with these processor enhancements.

MEMORY

Although Encore DVD lists its memory requirements as 256 megabytes of RAM, 512 megabytes is recommended to run Encore DVD simultaneously with Photoshop and After Effects. If you can afford 1 gigabytes or more of memory, go for it.

HARD DISK

Because DVD discs range from 4 to 18 gigabytes in size, large-capacity hard disks are a necessity for DVD authoring. Encore DVD requires ten gigabytes of available space. Note that available space is the disk space left over *after* installing the operating system, all software, fonts, and other material—it is not the capacity of the hard disk. Ten gigabytes will fill quickly, and realistically, 10 gigabytes of available space will support authoring one project or at most two projects concurrently. If you plan to do a fair amount of DVD authoring, have 60 gigabytes or more of available storage. Add additional storage such as a second hard disk or a disk array if you plan to edit video on the same machine.

DISPLAY AND VIDEO CARD

Between designing menus, constructing timelines, and simulation, you should have at least one large (1280 by 1024 pixels) monitor. Two monitors are highly recommended. With two displays, you can spread Encore DVD's windows out and quickly access items without having to close and reopen windows.

Your display card should support full color (referred to as "millions of color" or 24-bit color) at 1280 by 1024 pixels. The card should have at least 16 to 32 megabytes of video memory. If you plan to support two displays with a single card, I would recommend purchasing a card with 64 or 128 megabytes of video memory.

DVD-ROM DRIVE AND A SUPPORTED DVD BURNER

The software and additional content ships on a DVD, so you need a DVD-ROM drive. If you plan to create DVDs, you'll need a DVD drive that burns DVDs.

 See Adobe's Web site for an updated list of supported DVD burning drives: http://www.adobe.com/products/encore/systemreqs.html.

SOUND REQUIREMENTS

A stereo sound card is required to hear audio while previewing a project in Encore DVD. In addition, you should consider purchasing external stereo speakers or, if your sound card supports 5.1 surround sound, surround sound speakers.

 Although Encore DVD cannot encode 5.1 surround sound, it can import and preview surround sound audio encoded in another application. It can also write surround sound audio files when building a project.

Suggested Hardware

VIDEO CAMERA, VIDEO DECK

A CCD is a charged-coupled device, an electronic component behind the lens that records color and light information.

If you are producing video for DVDs, purchase or rent a three-CCD video camera equipped with Firewire and a high-speed cabling system for connecting video and storage equipment to computers. It is also known as Sony iLink or the IE1394 standard. Cameras with three CCDs take better video because they capture color and detail better than a camera with a single CCD.

If you own a video camera already, consider purchasing a video deck to capture the video from the camera. A video deck saves wear and tear on your camera and saves you the time of reconnecting your camera to the computer.

A video tripod with a smooth fluid head and level rounds out your camera kit. Although hand-held shots are great, they are not meant for all shots. If you videotape scenery, interviews, or other B roll, a level tripod gives you steady footage and smoother pans and tilts.

A PROFESSIONAL VIDEO NTSC OR PAL VIDEO MONITOR

You should always use a professional television monitor to preview your broadcast video project, even if your computer has action and title safe guides. If you plan to design wide screen menus, look into a video monitor that can switch between 4:3 and 16:9 aspect ratios.

DVD PLAYER

One or more set-top DVD players are crucial for proofing test discs. I recommend purchasing a cheap DVD player so you can test the low end of DVD set-top players in addition to the fancier Sony, Panasonic, or Pioneer player that you might already own. The Sony PlayStation 2 and Microsoft Xbox are also great proofing systems.

DIGITAL CAMERA AND SCANNER

A scanner is useful when you want to input paper sketches, flow charts, illustrations, and photographic prints, negatives, and positives. A digital camera is a great resource for taking photos quickly and transferring photos to Photoshop for embellishment.

The DVD Menu

A menu is the user interface for a DVD. It contains hotspots, which are called buttons. Buttons play video, go to additional menus, display text subtitles, or switch audio tracks. This chapter discusses both still and motion menus and the differences between the two.

This chapter presents the following topics.

* Menu structure
* Digital video and DVD menu design
* The differences between still and motion menus
* Types of menus
* Types of links

Menu Structure

To the viewer, a DVD menu appears to be a background image with buttons on top, but it is actually a single video frame without audio. As the user presses the arrows keys on the remote control, the selection moves among the buttons onscreen. The button's appearance changes as it is selected or activated. Pressing the Enter key activates a selected button and either goes to the button's link destination or executes a command, such as displaying subtitle text. Figure 2-1 shows the components of a menu.

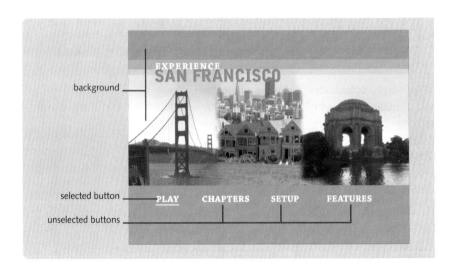

Figure 2-1: **A typical menu**

Buttons

Although buttons go to links or initiate commands, they need not look like buttons in a software application. A button can be any combination of image, shape, and text. Most DVDs use only text with a simple rollover, as shown in Table 2-1.

BUTTON STATES

A button has three unique states—Normal, Selected, and Activated—triggered by selecting one button, or another button, and engaging the button after selecting it. Table 2-1 shows how the states are shown onscreen with the subpicture and corresponding state colors from the menu's color set.

Table 2-1: **Button states from a one-color subpicture**

PLAY	**Normal** When a button is not selected.
PLAY	**Selected** A selection is made with the arrow keys on a remote or with the cursor if played on a computer.
PLAY	**Activated** Activation occurs when a button is selected and the viewer presses the Enter key on a remote or clicks on the button on a computer.

When Encore DVD builds the DVD, it flattens the buttons and the background into one videostream, so the viewer interacts with hotspots on the video. The following items create this interaction.

- *Highlight region.* The highlight region is not a visible image—it is a list of screen coordinates specifying where each button, or hotspot, is located. It is analogous to an HTML image map, but note that it's only rectangular.

- *Subpicture.* This graphic is used to create the selected and activated button states. You see a piece of it when you select or activate a button. Subpictures are analogous to an HTML rollover effect.

- *Color set.* This is a color palette containing 15 colors. Each color also has an optional level of transparency. These colors are used to colorize the subpicture to show a button's state. The palette is divided into three colors for the normal state and two groups of six colors for the selected and activated states.

- *Button routing.* This comprises the navigational paths between buttons that are followed when the arrow keys on a remote control are pressed. It is analogous to Tab key order on an HTML form.

- *Button order.* This is the numerical ordering of buttons. Pressing the number keys on a remote control selects buttons on the basis of their button number.

 In Encore DVD, you can specify that a button is automatically activated when it is selected. This is useful for touchscreen kiosks or for menus with more visually elaborate button states.

HIGHLIGHT REGION
The highlight region contains *x* and *y* coordinates that specify where buttons are and which portion of the subpicture to show for each button. Figure 2-2 is a repre-

sentation of a menu's highlight region, but note that the highlight region is not an image stored on the disc, nor do you create it in Encore DVD.

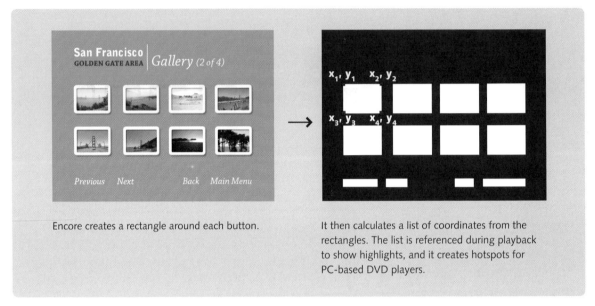

Encore creates a rectangle around each button.

It then calculates a list of coordinates from the rectangles. The list is referenced during playback to show highlights, and it creates hotspots for PC-based DVD players.

Figure 2-2: **Highlight region**

If you have ever created highlight regions in other applications, you will be glad to discover that you are spared this task in Encore DVD, which does this automatically.

SUBPICTURES

A subpicture is a four-color (2-bit) image composited on top of a DVD menu or timeline during playback. Subpictures serve two purposes. For menus, they are the highlight that appears when a button is selected or activated. For timelines, they are the subtitle text. In both situations, one color is used for a matte, and the remaining colors (up to three) are for the fill. In most cases, a menu subpicture is only two colors: one for the matte and the other for the fill.

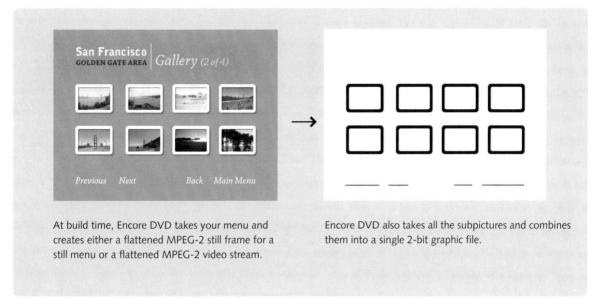

At build time, Encore DVD takes your menu and creates either a flattened MPEG-2 still frame for a still menu or a flattened MPEG-2 video stream.

Encore DVD also takes all the subpictures and combines them into a single 2-bit graphic file.

Figure 2-3: **Subpicture**

The rollover effect is created by the DVD player. The player shows the subpicture when the user selects or activates a button. The player can also change the color and opacity of the highlight so the selected state looks different from the activated state. When viewing this effect on an NTSC or a PAL television, it appears acceptable because television resolution is too low to show the aliasing. When viewed on a high-resolution computer display, the subpicture's crude aliasing is noticeable.

 NTSC is the television standard used in North America and Japan whereas PAL is used in Europe.

The rollover effect on a DVD menu is less flexible than is possible with a Web page or Flash file. These other media allow full-color effects such as smoothly colored glows or animated rollovers. DVD rollovers are a simple color change because DVD players (especially old ones) have limited processing power to display menus and video without crashing.

MENU COLOR SETS

A color set provides the color information for button highlights. It has 15 color options specified in red, green, and blue (RGB). Each option also has an opacity value.

 In addition to RGB, a color option can be specified by hue, saturation, and brightness.

See *Encore DVD Layer Naming Convention on page 171* for more information.

Within a set are a normal color group, and two highlight groups. Two things to notice are that all groups within a color set have a Color 1, Color 2, and Color 3 option and each of these have an opacity setting. The three colors correspond to the colors available to the subpicture. They also map to the Photoshop layers used to create the subpicture. The opacity setting allows for portions of a button highlight to be fully, partially, or not transparent.

	Color 1	Color 2	Color 3		
Normal Group This group is used for every button's normal state.	0%	0%	0%	PLAY HOME	Most DVD menus set the normal group to be fully transparent.
Highlight Group 1 Selected state colors	100%	100%	100%	LAY HOME	The Play button is selected and uses highlight group 1.
Highlight Group 1 Activated state colors	100%	100%	100%	PLAY HOME	When the Play button is activated, the colors change to the activated colors.
Highlight Group 2 Selected state colors	100%	100%	100%	PLAY HOME	The Home button is selected and uses highlight group 2.
Highlight Group 2 Activated state colors	100%	100%	100%	PLAY HOME	When the Home button is activated, the colors change to the activated colors.

Figure 2-4: **Menu color set**

By having three subpictures of similar color but varying levels of opacity, antialiasing for button highlights can be created.

The normal group is three colors for the unselected button state. In most menu designs, these colors aren't used and are set to be fully transparent. Whereas one button might use highlight group 1 and another button highlight group 2, all buttons on the menu will use the normal group for the unselected button state.

The highlight groups have three colors for both the selected and activated states. Because the activated state is only shown for a short period of time before the DVD advances to the button's link, there is the option to use the same color for both the selected and activated states. Having two groups provides two general color options for buttons. You can select either the first or second highlight group in the Button Properties palette.

 A menu can only have one color set. Although it can be changed iteratively during the authoring process, it cannot be changed during playback.

Encore DVD automatically generates a color set from a Photoshop file that follows the Encore DVD layer naming convention, or you can create a custom color set.

See Automatic Color Sets on page 144 for more information on automatic and custom menu color sets.

COMBINING THE SUBPICTURE, COLOR SET, AND HIGHLIGHT REGION

Although it might look like two or three unique graphics being swapped in and out while hovering over a button and activating it, only the single subpicture is dynamically colorized. Figure 2-5 shows how these elements are combined to create button states.

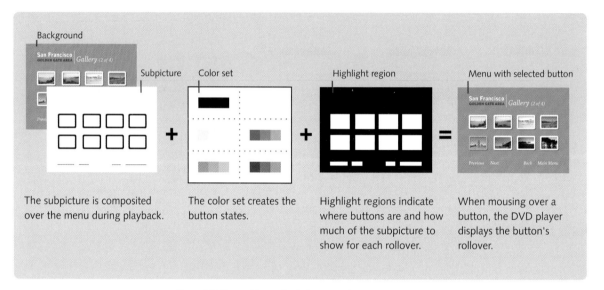

Figure 2-5: **Menu video and subpicture graphics**

DESIGNING SUBPICTURES
Although most DVD menu designers use only one color for the highlight, a multi-colored subpicture with a varied color set offers more design possibilities. If you are interested in knowing how to design subpictures in Encore DVD and Photoshop, see Chapter Six. It covers button design and highlights in more detail.

Table 2-2: **Subpicture examples**

NORMAL	SELECTED	ACTIVATED	EXPLANATION
Play	Play	Play	A single subpicture is used with different colors for the selected and activated states.
Play	Play	Play	The same effect as above, but instead of an underline, a copy of the text layer is used.
Play	Play	Play	Three subpictures are used with three colors for the selected and activated states.

BUTTON ROUTING

Button routing is the path designated between buttons. When a viewer presses the arrow keys on a remote control, the routing indicates which button is selected by pressing up, down, left, or right. Encore DVD can determine the routing automatically, or you can set the routing manually if your menu layout is more complicated.

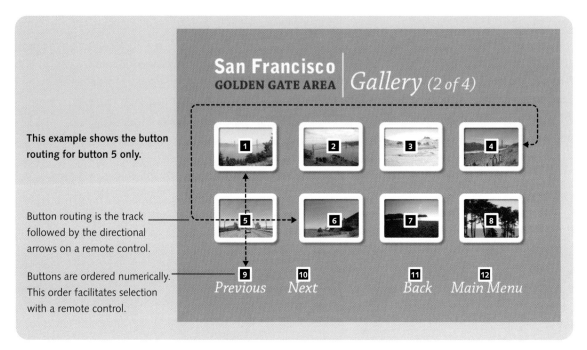

This example shows the button routing for button 5 only.

Button routing is the track followed by the directional arrows on a remote control.

Buttons are ordered numerically. This order facilitates selection with a remote control.

Figure 2-6: **Button routing and numbering**

Encore DVD has several methods for automatic routing.

- *Route up/down.* This option enables the up and down arrows on a DVD remote control to move between buttons.

- *Wrap around up/down.* This alters the routing so that the selection moves from a button at the bottom of one column to the button at the top of the same or next column.

- *Route left/right.* This option enables the left and right arrows on a DVD remote control to move between buttons.

- *Wrap around left/right.* This alters the routing so that the selection moves from a button at the end of one row to the first button in the same or next row.

Although Encore DVD can automatically calculate this path for you, on occasion, you will want to do this yourself. For instance, if you are designing a set of chapter menus, you will often want the routing between the chapter buttons to function separately from the routing between the Next, Previous and Main Menu buttons.

If your design is circular or does not adhere to a grid, automatic routing might not match your button layout. In these instances, disable automatic button routing and manually edit it.

Routing editing is covered in more detail in Button Routing on page 143.

BUTTON ORDERING

A DVD menu can have up to 36 buttons and each button is numbered. These numbers are helpful for choosing buttons with the number keys on a remote control. The number for each button is set in the Button Properties palette. If the menu has a 16:9 aspect ratio, only 18 buttons are allowed because two aspect ratios (4:3 and 16:9) are generated and the buttons need to display correctly when viewed in either aspect ratio.

When importing a Photoshop file as a menu, Encore DVD assigns the number 1 to the lowest button layer set and sequentially assigns higher numbers to the layer sets above it. Although Encore DVD initially assigns numbers this way, you can change the numbers to whatever you like through the Button Properties palette. These changes will be preserved even if you edit the menu in Photoshop again and return to Encore DVD.

DEFAULT BUTTON

Every menu has a default button that is selected when the menu is initially displayed. For example, the main menu for a film DVD would mostly likely have the Play Movie button as the default.

 If you want a different button to be selected when returning to a menu, set the Override property for the item linking to the button.

Digital Video and DVD Design

This section discusses the frame aspect ratio, resolution, and pixel aspect ratio for the NTSC and PAL video formats. Understanding the nature of these formats will make you a more technically savvy menu designer.

Video Formats

Encore DVD can create video discs for either the NTSC or the PAL television standard. NTSC is the video broadcast standard used in the United States, Canada, and Japan. PAL is the video broadcast standard in Europe, but is used elsewhere too.

NTSC video plays at 29.97 frames per second (fps) at a resolution of 720 by 480 pixels. PAL video plays at 25 frames per second at a resolution of 720 by 576 pixels. Although NTSC has a slightly higher frame rate, PAL has slightly greater resolution and is closer to the frame rate of film, which is 24 frames per second. The two formats also have different pixel aspect ratios, which is discussed later.

 A single DVD cannot support both PAL and NTSC standards. If you need to author for both standards, create separate PAL and NTSC projects.

MPEG-2

MPEG, pronounced m-peg, stands for Moving Picture Experts Group. MPEG is a collection of international standards for digitally compressing audio and visual information. The compression and decompression algorithm is often called a codec (compressor/decompressor). Compression is the method of shrinking the file size, and decompression is the method of reinterpreting the compressed file for playback. The MPEG collection of standards includes MPEG-1, MPEG-2, and MPEG-4.

DVDs use a strict form of MPEG-2. The strict rules define the frame size, frame rate, aspect ratio, GOP (group of pictures) length, and maximum bitrate. The frame sizes, rates, and aspect ratios allowed are listed in Table 2-3 on page 29. In DVD authoring, bitrate is widely defined as the amount of data in megabits (Mbits) read from the disc per second. The maximum bitrate allowed for a DVD is 9.8 megabits per second. Bitrate is calculated from the video stream and all audio and subtitle streams. Video streams are the largest, followed by audio, and subtitle streams are the smallest of the streams. It is probably best to keep the bitrate under 9 megabits per second just so there is a little headroom for the player. Although there is not a set minimum bitrate for video, 2 megabits per second or less produces very poor video and should be avoided.

Like many digital video compression methods, MPEG-2 employs intraframe and interframe compression. Intraframe compression reduces the size of a single frame, whereas interframe compression looks at similarities across a range of frames to shrink file size. A GOP is the smallest range of frames in an MPEG-2 video stream and is composed of frames with more detail (I frames) and lesser detail (P and B frames). P frames contain more information than B frames. MPEG-2 video streams that are DVD-legal have GOPs that are fifteen frames long.

The three important things to remember about MPEG-2 are: GOP placement, bitrates, and bit budgeting. Exceeding the bitrate can cause a DVD player to crash, and using high bitrates for all content on the disc can consume all the allocated space for the disc and leave you with no room for additional content.

GOP PLACEMENT

Knowing where GOPs are placed in a video stream is important when you set chapter points for a timeline in Encore DVD. Since chapter points can only exist on the boundaries of a GOP, there are times when the exact frame you want to mark as a chapter is not available because it is within fifteen frames of the nearest GOP or another chapter.

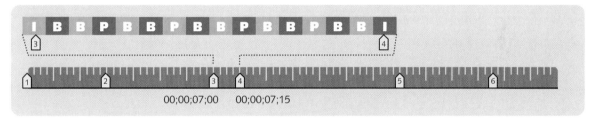

Figure 2-7: **Legal locations for chapter points in an MPEG-2 DVD-videostream**

 If you set chapter markers before transcoding video to MPEG-2, Encore DVD will attempt to place GOPs where chapters occur.

CONSTANT AND VARIABLE BITRATES

With the constant bitrate compression method, the data rate is held constant regardless of what is being compressed. Portions that do not require the full data rate waste space, and portions that require more than the full data rate suffer in quality. By contrast, the variable bitrate method analyzes content in multiple passes and varies the data rate based upon specified data rate targets. Portions that need detail are given the maximum amount of bandwidth, and less detailed sequences are given lower amounts.

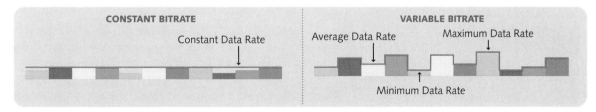

Figure 2-8: **Comparing constant and variable bitrates**

BIT BUDGETING

For short video clips such as an introductory animation or a motion menu, use a high bitrate, since it doesn't have additional audio streams and the short length ensures that alot of disc space isn't consumed. In addition, video quality often benefits from a higher bitrate. If you have one long video clip (an hour or more) with multiple audio streams or several video clips of 10 minutes or more, use a smaller bitrate so that when audio and video bitrates are calculated together there is enough bandwidth available.

Frame Aspect Ratio

Frame aspect ratio is the proportional relationship between a video's width and height. Frame aspect ratio is a relative measurement, and it should not be confused with resolution, which is absolute. Nearly all NTSC and PAL video is created with a 4:3 aspect ratio. This means the width is one-third longer than the height. Your television set is most likely a 4:3 television screen. The 4:3 aspect ratio is referred to as the "standard" because it has been used for decades.

More televisions now support high-definition video (HD), which has a 16:9 aspect ratio. This aspect ratio is referred to as "widescreen" because it is closer to film aspect ratios. Although the DVD-Video specification and mini-DV camcorders do not support high-definition video, they do support standard definition video (SD) with a 16:9 aspect ratio.

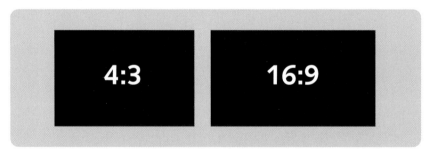

Figure 2-9: **DVD-Video aspect ratios**

Video footage at 16:9 is created by a video camera with a native 16:9 CCD or with an anamorphic lens adapter. The anamorphic process compresses the video image horizontally to a 4:3 video file that is stored on the DVD. During the production process, you flag the video as anamorphic and the DVD player uncompresses the video back to the 16:9 aspect ratio during playback. If the viewer owns a 16:9 television or watches the DVD on a computer screen, the video is shown in 16:9. If the television is 4:3, the DVD player will letterbox the video, that is, put horizontal black bars across the top and bottom so the video fills the television screen.

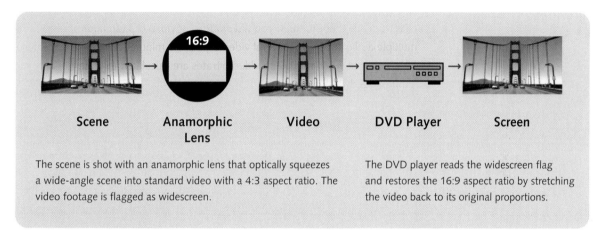

Scene   **Anamorphic Lens**   **Video**   **DVD Player**   **Screen**

The scene is shot with an anamorphic lens that optically squeezes a wide-angle scene into standard video with a 4:3 aspect ratio. The video footage is flagged as widescreen.

The DVD player reads the widescreen flag and restores the 16:9 aspect ratio by stretching the video back to its original proportions.

Figure 2-10: **The anamorphic process**

Resolution

Resolution is the number of pixels in an image. Resolution is often described as the number of horizontal pixels by the number of vertical pixels; for example, 720 by 480 for NTSC and 720 by 576 for PAL. Whereas DVD-Video supports low (352 by 240 for NTSC and 352 by 288 for PAL) and high video resolutions, Encore DVD supports only high resolution.

Pixel Aspect Ratio

Pixels (picture elements) are the tiny squares of color arranged on a two-dimensional grid that form an image. The aspect ratio of a single video pixel is its width relative to its height. One would imagine that video pixels would be perfectly square like the pixels on a computer screen. This could not be further from the truth! The NTSC and PAL digital video formats have rectangular (also referred to as nonsquare) pixels. A 4:3 NTSC video is 10 percent narrower than a computer's square pixel, whereas a 4:3 PAL video is roughly seven percent wider than a computer's square pixel. These formats have rectangular pixels because of recent broadcast technology. NTSC video used to be 640 by 480 or 648 by 486. In the 1990s, the NTSC D1 video standard was defined to be 720 by 486. By packing more discreet blocks of resolution, more detail was made available. Unfortunately when digital video and DVD were defined, 720 by 480 was considered preferable to 720 by 486. Table 2-3 lists the resolutions and pixel aspect ratios for 4:3 and 16:9 NTSC and PAL video.

 If you import D1 footage at 720 by 486, Encore DVD crops three pixels from the top and bottom to make it compliant with the 720 by 480 resolution of DVDs.

Table 2-3: **Resolution for NTSC and PAL television standards**

TELEVISION STANDARD	FPS	RESOLUTION	PIXEL ASPECT RATIO
NTSC DV/DVD Standard (4:3)	29.97	720 x 480	0.9 x 1.0
NTSC DV/DVD Widescreen (16:9)	29.97	720 x 480	1.2 x 1.0
PAL DV/DVD Standard (4:3)	25	720 x 576	1.0666 x 1.0
PAL DV/DVD Widescreen (16:9)	25	720 x 576	1.422 x 1.0

When designing DVD menus and still graphics in Photoshop, you need to size files to accommodate pixel aspect ratio differences between video and computer screens. For more information, see the section on Encore DVD layer naming convention in Chapter Six.

When you acquire footage from a DV camera, it will follow the settings listed above. You can directly import this footage and use it in a timeline as a background for a motion menu. If you are creating animation, see if your animation software can output a file at this resolution. If it cannot, you can follow the size requirements of DVD-Video for still images, render your animation at this resolution, and use a program like After Effects or Premiere to resize your animation.

DVD Links and User Operations

When designing DVD navigation, you are creating links between items. For example, you create links between buttons on a menu and chapter points in a timeline. The DVD also has global links that are accessed from a DVD remote control. This section is an overview on the types of links available in DVD authoring. For more information on designing user-friendly and intuitive navigation, see "Interaction and Navigation" in Chapter Four. If you are anxious to start setting links, see "Setting Button Properties and Links" in Chapter Seven.

Six properties facilitate linking: the First Play, remote control Title button, remote control Menu button, Link, Override, and End Action. Everything except End Action is a menu:button, timeline:chapter point, or Not Set.

End Action also follows the menu:button and timeline:chapter point formats, but instead of a null value of Not Set, it has null value of Stop. Additional link properties, such as which audio track or subtitle text track to play, also can be set.

First Play

The first play is the first image shown when a DVD begins to play. In most DVDs, this is the FBI message that warns against illegally distributing the DVD's content. If you are not developing a DVD that requires this warning, the first play could be a company logo, or even a main menu as on the disc included with this book. First plays can be menus or they can be timelines.

 Encore DVD, by default, uses the first menu or timeline created as the first play. You can set it to something else by choosing File > Set First Play.

Remote Control Title Button

The Title button is on nearly every remote control and, generally speaking, is labelled Title, but occasionally it is labeled Home, or Top Menu. This property is set once for the entire disc and can be accessed from any menu or timeline. The Title button is best set to the disc's main menu or an introductory video segment that leads to the main menu. Think of it as being similar to the Home button on a Web page that sends you to the Web site's home page.

REMOTE CONTROL MENU BUTTON

The Menu button is also on nearly every remote control and is almost always labeled Menu. This is a timeline property and it sends the viewer back to the menu that is playing the current video or to a menu that allows the viewer to navigate to another item on the disc.

LINK

Link is a button property. Buttons link to other menus and to chapters within a timeline. This property contains either a menu:button combination or a timeline:chapter point combination. It is what the DVD player advances to when a button is activated.

END ACTION

An end action occurs at the end of a timeline or when a menu "times out." When a timeline completes playing, the DVD player will advance to the destination specified by the timeline's End Action property, which should normally link back to the menu that called the timeline. However, a timeline's end action could also link to the next related timeline.

A menu can have an end action, but it cannot hold or loop forever. It must have a duration (still menu) or be looped a number of times (motion menu). If the menu holds or loops forever, the End Action property is ignored. If you are designing a DVD public or tradeshow kiosk, you might want to set all the menus to time out and use an end action to reset the kiosk to an introductory video or menu. You can also create interactive quizzes that time out with the End Action, Duration and Loop Number properties.

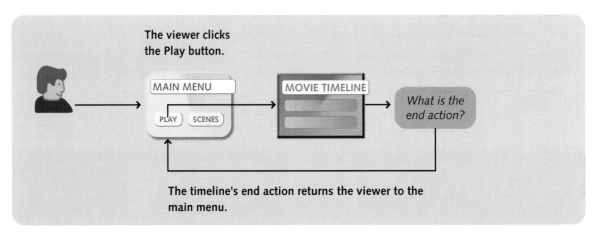

Figure 2-11: **End action example**

OVERRIDE

The First Play, Link, and End Action properties have a companion Override property, which replaces the end action of a timeline or menu from another link or end action. The following example illustrates how an override works.

You are designing a DVD with three lessons that are three separate timelines. The Lessons menu contains four buttons, one for each lesson and one to play all the lessons. For each timeline, you create a link between each lesson: Lesson 1 links to Lesson 2, and Lesson 2 links to Lesson 3. On the Lessons menu, each button links to a menu, but each lesson button's Override property links back to the Lesson menu and selects the button for the next lesson. The All button links to Lesson 1 and plays the remaining lessons as expected.

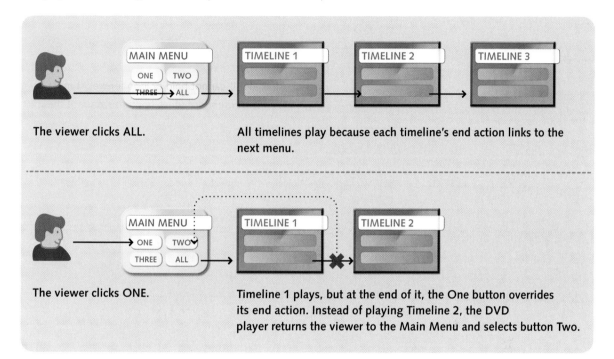

Figure 2-12: **Override example**

The Override property is perhaps Encore DVD's most powerful navigational feature because with it, you can design smarter navigation that would require scripting or the creation of additional timelines in other applications.

 In Encore DVD, the Remote Control Menu and Title button properties do not have a companion Override property.

User Operations

A disc, menu, and timeline all have user operation settings that permit or prohibit interaction between the user and the functions on a DVD remote control. For example, most Hollywood discs prohibit all user operations until after the FBI warning.

Timelines and Playlists

Timelines

Menus are the interface to timelines on a DVD. Timelines contain the video content you shot, edited, and imported into Encore DVD, as well as additional audio and subtitle tracks. A DVD can have up to 99 timelines.

In Encore DVD, there are one video track, eight audio tracks, and thirty-two subtitle tracks per timeline. Chapters within a timeline serve as shortcuts to scenes within the content. Upon completion, all timelines have an End Action link that returns the viewer to the menu viewed prior to playing the timeline.

Playlists

A playlist is a selection of timelines that play in sequential order. The End Actions for each timeline in a playlist are ignored by the program, and then one End Action is observed for the entire playlist.

Creating playlists allows for multiple paths through a DVD. For example, a video production company organizes its projects on a DVD by animation and live action, as well as corporate and music video. Certain reels would fall under animation or live action, but the selections for corporate and music video could contain both animation and live action pieces. In Figure 2-13, the same content is referenced in multiple playlists to create alternative presentations.

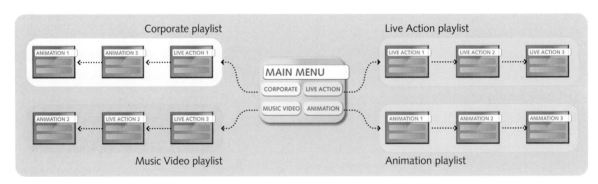

Figure 2-13: **Playlists**

The Difference between Still and Motion Menus

There are two types of DVD menus, still and motion. A still menu is a single video frame without audio. It can be held indefinitely, waiting for user interaction, or it can time out and trigger an action. A motion menu, by contrast, is full-motion video with or without audio or is a single video frame with audio.

Still Menus

A still menu is a static frame of video with no motion or audio associated with it. It is simpler than a motion menu and is easier to create. Motion menus can be held onscreen indefinitely, or they can play for a set duration of time and then go somewhere else on the DVD (Table 2-13). Still menus are often designed in Photoshop, but Encore DVD has a Menu Editor.

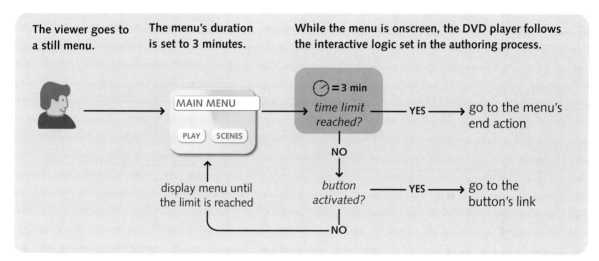

Figure 2-14: **Still menu timing options**

Motion Menus

A motion menu in Encore DVD can be one of several combinations of still or motion video and audio.

* A still background with audio
* A motion video background with no audio
* A motion video background with audio

Motion menus are different from still menus with regard to timing. A still menu has only a Duration field, whereas a motion menu has the Duration field and two properties for looping: a loop point and the number of loops.

Chapters 8 and 9 have tutorials for creating motion menus.

In Encore DVD, a still menu that has video chapter buttons becomes a motion menu when the Animate Buttons property is turned on because Encore DVD then renders live video from each chapter point into each button area. The Duration property is used for the duration of the video referenced for each button. For more information on video chapter buttons, see Chapter Eight.

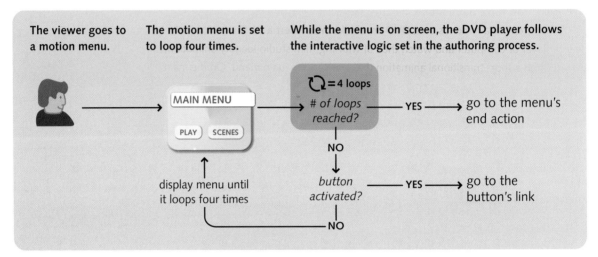

The viewer goes to a motion menu.

The motion menu is set to loop four times.

While the menu is on screen, the DVD player follows the interactive logic set in the authoring process.

Figure 2-15: **Motion menu timing options**

More elaborate motion menus are created with Adobe After Effects, the most widely used motion graphics and compositing application for film and video. Chapter Nine has information on how to use After Effects for advanced motion menu creation.

Types of Menus

A typical DVD has a dozen menus. Most of these menus follow certain patterns of use that can be generically described and categorized. The DVD-Video specification defines a few types of menus: root, scene, subtitle, audio, and angle menus. Angle menus, by the way, are not possible in Encore DVD 1.5 because Encore DVD does not support multiple angles. Although you will undoubtedly create one or more of these menus, they do not necessarily give you a complete idea of the types of menus that will suit your content and your navigation needs.

For this reason, I provide a list of menus that are typically found in a DVD project, and I explain how they can be tailored for different purposes. All of these menus are not necessarily part of the DVD-Video specification, but knowing what they are and when to use them will help you prepare content and design DVD navigation.

Main Menus

A Web site's home page, after the introductory animation, provides links to the site's content. Main menus on a DVD are similar. You insert a DVD into your set top player or computer and watch the FBI warning, film studio identity animation, and often a short transitional animation that leads to the main menu. On the main menu is a button to play the entire movie from start to finish, a button to special features, a button to chapter selections, and a button that links to a DVD configuration menu. The main menu is often the root menu. When you press the Title or Menu buttons on a DVD remote control, you will often see the main menu.

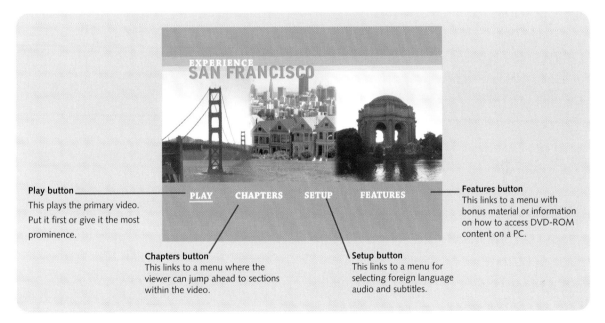

Play button
This plays the primary video. Put it first or give it the most prominence.

Chapters button
This links to a menu where the viewer can jump ahead to sections within the video.

Setup button
This links to a menu for selecting foreign language audio and subtitles.

Features button
This links to a menu with bonus material or information on how to access DVD-ROM content on a PC.

Figure 2-16: **Sample main menu design**

Although a DVD does not require a main menu—a DVD can simply have a video that plays immediately—it is highly recommended that you provide one to viewers so they can access the content areas of the DVD. Later in the book, I'll show you how to organize a main menu for simplicity and ease of use.

Secondary Menus

Nearly all menus other than the main menu are secondary menus. These menus present links to subsets of the DVD's content, offer options for configuring the viewer's DVD experience, or present content in and of itself, such as slide shows.

> *All secondary menus should have a link back to the main menu. When there are more than two levels of menus, provide buttons that go up a level from the current secondary menu.*

CHAPTER SELECTION MENU

A chapter or scene selection menu contains buttons that link to sequentially numbered chapter markers in a timeline. A DVD timeline can have up to 99 markers, so multiple chapter selection menus are possible. In this case, each menu will have Next and Previous buttons to switch between scene menus in addition to the chapter buttons.

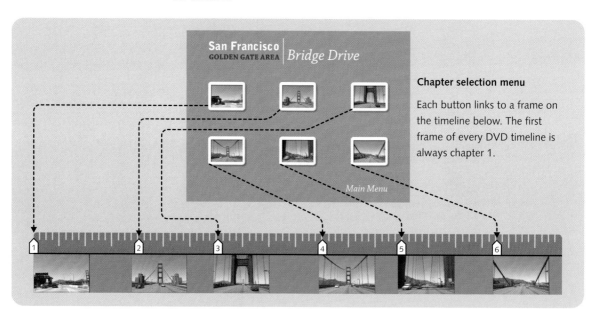

Chapter selection menu

Each button links to a frame on the timeline below. The first frame of every DVD timeline is always chapter 1.

Figure 2-17: **Chapter selection menu**

FEATURES MENU

When viewing a DVD from a major studio, a special features menu often contains links to trailers, a behind-the-scenes documentary, slide shows, help, DVD-ROM content information, or supplemental audio tracks with narration from a director or actor. Additional menus could fall under the special features menu—it really depends on your content. If you are developing a DVD for another purpose, such as education, sales, or training, you can use elements of this type of menu to present slide shows, provide interviews with teachers, and present interactive quizzes.

SLIDE SHOW MENU

Slide show menus are photo presentations with underactivity. Some DVD authors prefer to present photographs in a timeline. The advantages are that the viewers advance the images and an audio track can accompany the photos. Slide shows with menus offer the viewer more navigational control, and the viewer can advance through the photos quickly. Chapter Six presents several ideas on how to combine timeline and menu-based slide shows to create a more compelling viewer experience.

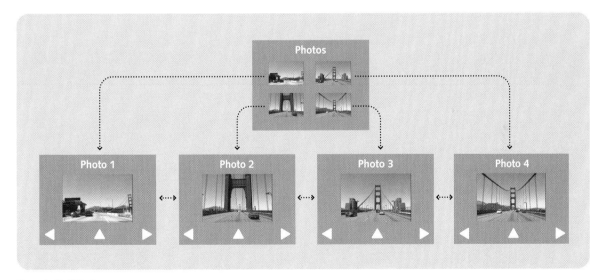

Figure 2-18: **Slide show menus**

DISC SETUP MENU

The Setup menu contains links to display subtitle text for foreign languages or to play auxiliary audio tracks for foreign languages. The menu lists the languages that are available for subtitles and as audio tracks. Selection of these links does not necessarily play the movie with the subtitles immediately. Often the designer will create a nearly identical menu with the word on next to the recently chosen subtitle or audio selection.

 Subtitle text is cheaper to produce than audio narration and occupies significantly less disc space. It depends on the budget, schedule, and available resources.

HELP MENU

Most DVDs are simple and straightforward enough that they do not need a Help menu. If you plan to provide a lot of content on the disc or are creating a set of DVDs, you might want to create a help menu. This menu can link to informative video tours of the DVD or provide a screen-to-screen instructional overview of the DVD with text.

Research, Interaction Design, and Usability

The three disciplines listed in the title of this chapter help you craft the viewer's experience when watching and interacting with a DVD. This chapter is a primer on how to plan the interface and apply good interface design principles.

This chapter presents the following topics.

- Conducting research
- Designing interaction and navigation
- Prototyping
- Usability testing

Process

When someone mentions process, others tend to yawn, myself included. Joking aside, a well-defined process shortens development and improves the quality of the overall project. Although the DVD production process covers many steps between inception and the shiny disc, I'm going to cover only the interface and visual design stages required for designing menus. This chapter covers interaction design, but Figure 3-1 on page 36 also shows the DVD authoring process.

When to Conduct Research, Do Design, and Test for Usability

You might wonder why I am covering user research and interaction design since most DVDs are fairly simple—one to two menus and perhaps one video. That may be true of some menus, but the vast majority of A-title Hollywood DVDs have a dozen or more menus and as many video segments. Training, sales, and education DVDs can be even more complex. The question to ask yourself is how complicated is the project going to be and what really needs to be done to make sure the disc is easy to use. If you are putting a lot of menus on timelines on the DVD, you will want to consider following these practices.

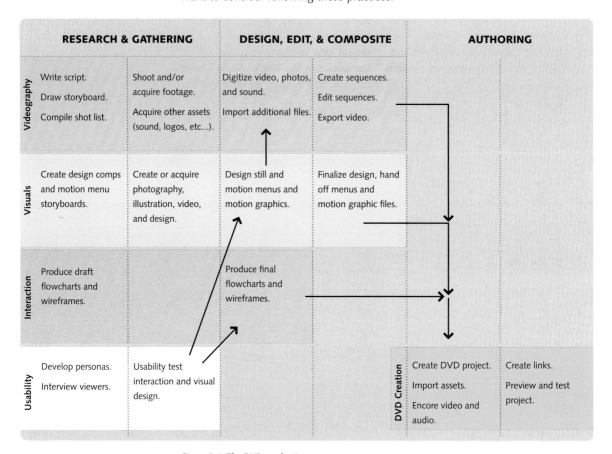

Figure 3-1: **The DVD production process**

Selling Process to Clients

If your client thinks a menu with a few buttons is all that is needed for a large DVD of video training materials, you might need to educate the client and tell them not all DVD projects are that simple.

For example, in the software industry, companies that make the effort to understand their users and the user's environment enjoy high customer loyalty. They achieve this through user-centered design (a development methodology in which the customers' needs are put first). Although this is not a radical notion for someone in the design or retail industry, it was a radical idea for many software companies in the 1980s. And if I have not mentioned it yet, designing DVDs is very much like designing software. The more you understand the audience and the content you are presenting to them, the easier it is for them to navigate the disc. If they find your work user friendly and enjoyable, you gain repeat business, referrals, and good will.

User Research

Gather Requirements

The first step is to gather requirements from the client. You need to know the subject of the project, the audience, the method of delivery, the budget, and the schedule. I will cover how to understand your client and your client's client, the viewer. If you are creating DVDs primarily for event videography, this step will be fairly straightforward, and you can streamline a few of these steps. If you are a consultant for hire, the steps will help you as you move from project to project.

Understand the Client

You should receive the majority of project information during the initial conversations with the client. For example, the tourism bureau of San Francisco wants to develop a city guide on DVD. They plan to play the DVD in hotels and sell the DVD in tourist bureaus. The DVD will have virtual city tours, interactive maps, and printed guides on the DVD-ROM portion of the disc. Their goal is to have the disc completed and replicated in 6 months. With this information in hand, you know:

- The client—the tourism bureau of San Francisco.

- The project and scope—a city guide on San Francisco for tourists.

- The audience—tourists who are visiting San Francisco.

- The schedule—6 months.

If you do not receive this information initially, ask for it. If the client is prepared, you will receive a Request for Proposal (RFP), a creative brief, or a one-page treatment, of which outline the project goals, the scope, the content, and the schedule. An RFP is the most detailed of the three. It is your task to read this document, reply with a proposed budget and revised schedule, and perhaps pitch a few ideas on how to complete the project.

You might not want to show mock-ups because some clients will take your sketches and farm the idea out to someone who will work for less money. Whether or not to include sketches depends on the RFP requirements and your relationship with the client. If you have an established relationship, this is not a problem. If the client is new, show previous work; if the RFP requires a few sketches, keep them at the conceptual and wire frame level. Never overdeliver.

 A questionnaire is located on the DVD-ROM in the Usability and Research folder.

Making Bad Clients Better

Perhaps you do work for hire and you have the best client list in the world. If so, you are lucky and you should write a book and share your secrets. However, if you are new to world of working with clients, here is a short list of how to make bad clients better.

- *Establish goals.* Ask for a well written RFP or a clear definition of the project scope in a creative brief, storyboard, or outline.

- *Be proactive.* You need to have them put you in touch with the right people, and have them get you what you need—whether it be content or a check!

- *Set realistic expectations.* This is even more important if they are looking for a quick turn around.

- *Frame the discussion.* While it is appropriate to be critical, discourage vague feedback like "make it jazzier, greener, or cool." Ask for qualifications and be receptive.

Understand the Viewer (the Client's Client)

The most obvious way to understand viewers is to talk to them. You learn what viewers need and what makes sense to them. Spending just one afternoon and talking to four people will often save you time and increase the project's chances

for success. Testing is shortened and further design and testing can often be eliminated because you are not designing in the dark.

Define the Audience

Once you know the nature of the project, find viewers who are likely to watch the
DVD. Before you begin recruiting, however, work with the client to develop a list
of personas or user profiles. Personas are fictional characters who best represent
the audience. Give them names, give them a story, and create a simple chart listing
the items listed in Figure 3-2. Then use these personas to recruit viewers who fit
the description. Often you can base personas on real people you interview, or the
persona can be a composite of several people.

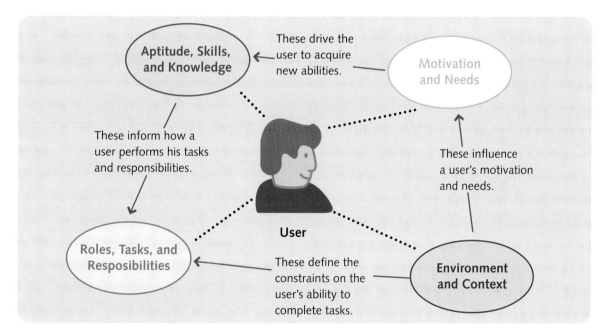

Figure 3-2: **A persona**

One important persona characteristic is how the user will view the disc. Will the
user be watching the disc on a computer, on a television, or on both? I ask this
because the way users interact with DVDs is noticeably different between the two
platforms. On a computer, the user uses the mouse to point at and click on buttons. Although most software DVD players support keyboard navigation, most
users rely on the mouse. By contrast, viewing a DVD on a set-top DVD player is

more constrained because the user has to use the arrow buttons on a remote control. These buttons do not give the same immediate access to buttons. More importantly, these buttons follow the routing that is designated during the authoring process. Although the authoring algorithms in Encore DVD do a great job, they might not work perfectly for complicated, circular button layouts. Therefore, it is important to view the button routing before burning the disc and to review the routing with viewers later in usability tests.

Keep your personas in mind when discussing features, design, and content. For example, Kay is a school teacher from Maine who wants to learn about cultural developments in San Francisco during the 1960s. She represents 30 percent of the audience. To accommodate this persona, you would want to include a brief segment on the Haight-Ashbury neighborhood or the area in North Beach around City Lights bookstore.

"Know your audience before you design" is the best advice I can give you. Designing with user research makes happier viewers. It also sets you apart from the competition, is something you can charge for, and makes you a better designer.

SCREENING PEOPLE TO INTERVIEW
Now that you know who will be using the DVD, you need to screen for real people who match the audience criteria and will talk with you. Talking with people who do not match the criteria does not fulfill your research needs. For instance, I would not interview many San Francisco residents for the DVD travel guide because although they might suggest wonderful places to visit, they do not have the same needs and experiences as the first-time San Francisco visitor.

An effective screening questionnaire will:

- Determine whether a person matches the audience criteria by collecting demographic information that qualifies potential subjects. Initial questions should be written so that people that do not match the audience criteria are eliminated quickly.

- Collect information regarding a subject's experience, attitudes, and affinities. This information helps researchers and designers understand a subject's responses during an interview or a test session.

   A screening questionnaire is located on the DVD-ROM in the Usability and Research folder.

Conduct the Interview

WHO TO BRING

In most cases you can conduct the interviews by yourself. If you are talking with only one person, an additional person is acceptable if you need someone dedicated to taking notes while you are talking or if you need someone to handle a video camera. More than two people is often overwhelming, so bring no more than two people (and never go over five) when interviewing three to four people at the same time. If more than one person wants to take part, rotate them in as the note taker.

It is a great idea to bring team members and clients on interviews because they gain insights that they would not gain from your report. Their first-hand experience can sometimes be a rude awakening, humbling, and, at best, eye opening. Their participation in the research and usability process makes it easier when it comes to getting agreements on important design decisions. You should, however, make it clear that they are there to observe and take notes—you are facilitating the interview. If they want to ask questions, they need to do it at the end and never interrupt. If they want to facilitate, switch off between interviews.

TELL THEM YOU WANT THEIR OPINION

When you begin, tell the viewer you want their candid opinion and advice. Let them know that everything is welcome and that they do not need to hold anything back. They can be as positive or negative as they want. All the advice they give will help create a better product. Tell them that you are there to listen and that you will encourage them to talk more if it is required.

GET CONSENT

When working on a commercial product, not only do people have to be willing to talk to you, but they have to give you permission, and sometimes they have to agree to keep what they have learned confidential—especially if you are testing a product that has competition. This is done by signing a consent form. By signing the form, the viewer understands the following points.

* The interview is for research and development purposes only. The information they share with you will be kept confidential and will not be used for marketing or other public use.

- They are free to stop the discussion at any time and they are not obligated to answer any questions they do not know or do not feel comfortable answering.

- They agree to keep the information they have learned from the discussion strictly confidential and not to discuss the product with third parties.

Have two copies on hand for each participant. Have them sign both copies, and then sign both copies yourself. Keep one and give the other copy to the participant.

 A consent form is on the DVD-ROM in the Usability and Research folder.

LET THE VIEWER DO THE TALKING

I refer to this as talking and not interviewing, because talking is more informal. You want the viewer to know that you are listening. Interviewing implies you are there to ask a lot of questions. Talking implies there will be a conversation. Although you might need to encourage the viewer to talk, you will learn more about the viewer if you listen and let the viewer talk more. It sounds simple, but it is rarely done!

KEEP THE DISCUSSION OPEN

Rather than lead with pointed questions on specific content planned for the DVD, ask the viewer qualitative questions like:

- What do you expect from the DVD?
- What do you need from it?
- What would you find valuable?

Pointed questions force people to say Yes or No and do not encourage long responses that yield the more important information. If you need straight answers, ask them later. If the viewer gives you a straight answer to a qualitative question, ask them to explain it—if something stinks, you need to know why.

Also, do not pose questions that imply a value judgement on your part. Appearing partial skews what the viewer will say. You are after the viewer's candid opinion.

ASK THE VIEWER TO COLLABORATE

Another way to learn from viewers is to ask them to design and collaborate with you. When they begin to describe something, ask them to sketch it for you. While they sketch, do not ask questions, but be quiet and offer encouragement. Even if you understand the design, keep listening and ask them to walk you through their explanations. Remember that the longer they talk, the more chances you have to learn new insights. If people do not feel comfortable sketching in front of you, give them a red pen and a sketch of the design. Ask them to improve it.

PHOTOS AND RECORDING

Bring a camera, and ask if you can take a photo. Tell them it is for research purposes only—it is *not* for public use. Add that having a photo helps you link your notes to what they say and that you need proof of your research. Do this at the end of the talk. In my experience, over the course of the talk, you build a rapport with the person and they do not mind having their photo taken. If anyone does not want to have their photo taken, respect their decision, and thank them for their time.

Recording the conversation on mini-DV or on a tape recorder can certainly help you with your notes and help if you are creating a presentation. If this is required, make sure you ask permission and make sure that the consent form states that they understand that the conversation might be recorded for research purposes only. Again, it is OK if they decline, just be sure to be taking notes.

THANK THE VIEWERS FOR THEIR TIME

When the time is up, thank the person for his time. Tell him that his opinion and advice has been helpful and that you value his involvement. Give him a business card and tell him that if he has any additional thoughts to feel free to e-mail you. It is also customary to pay the person for his time. Fifty dollars is an adequate amount for an hour of time. If you cannot offer a cash stipend, offer a small gift. In my experience, I have given users gift certificates and sometimes a tchotcheke (a cool item such as an "insider" T-shirt that was made for the development team). Leave them with a good impression, and you can come back to them when it is time to test your project.

WORKING WITH EXTERNAL AUDIENCES

If you are designing for an audience that is external to the client (a consumer, a corporate customer, a partner, or an investor) ask the client whether she has people in mind for the project. Often you can call people from a customer list or meet with someone the client knows. If she does not have these people handy, hiring a research recruitment firm can help you find people who match the user profiles.

WORKING WITH INTERNAL AUDIENCES

If you are designing for an audience that is internal to your company, the purpose of usability research and testing is the same as if you are creating a product for consumers. You need to find internal users who are most likely to benefit from the project and interview them. Scheduling time for interviews is significantly easier and cheaper than working with a recruiting agency because members of your audience may sit on the same floor as you. If you do not know the people personally, ask the manager of the audience who to interview. At Adobe, when we run practice usability tests, we advertise through mailing lists and post signs in the break and mail rooms.

If you are an outside consultant brought in to design material for an internal audience, you will need to ask the client to provide a list of names of employees to interview. Suggest to them that they advertise the interviews and tests internally. When you make contact with an internal audience, include them throughout the research and testing process and ask them whether they can recommend other employees for interviews.

WORKING WITH EVENT VIDEOGRAPHY CLIENTS

If you are an event videographer and produce DVDs for clients, your client *is* the audience, or at least an important part of it. Because you are creating the same project with slight variations, you do not need to do testing or research for every job. I would recommend that you extensively test your product at first and then do informal testing each time you introduce a new service.

Tailor your services to suit the majority of clients' needs. For instance, one client wants video that plays once the disc is inserted; another wants chapter points, motion menus, slide shows, or subtitles. Ask the client what media they have available or are willing to pay to have produced and show them what DVD authoring services you offer. Consider creating package deals and be ready to show clients examples of previous discs you have created for other clients. Like all projects, this can be an educational process.

GET TO KNOW THE PROJECT'S CONTENT

Although expert knowledge of the project's subject matter is not required, a general understanding helps you talk about it with clients and viewers, helps you design better navigation, and helps you design visuals that are relevant and appropriate to the audience.

CREATE A SCRAP BOOK

Usually when I begin any design project, I create a folder of material related to it. For example, if I were producing the travel guide DVD, I would go online, read book reviews of travel guides, and do searches on travelling to the San Francisco Bay area. Anything that interests me, I bookmark, save as a PDF file, and print. From there I would go to a book store and look for the books I found on the Internet, and I might buy a few. In addition, I look for documentaries on San Francisco, visit tourist information centers, and ask the staff what questions tourists frequently ask. I always have a camera ready to take pictures of things that might relate to the project. All of this goes into the folder.

WATCH THE VIDEO OR BE A PART OF IT

It should be obvious that you should watch the video and take notes. Look at the log notes and ask the editor for a dub so you can watch the material again and again. Look for small clips that you can meaningfully use in motion menu design or in a title sequence for the DVD's string of first play video. If you do not have access to the source tapes, schedule time to view them, write down the time codes, and create log notes for the clips you want to use in your designs. Then have the editor digitize and deliver them to you.

If the video has not been shot, you can play a crucial role because you have talked to viewers and read up on the subject, and you might have ideas you would like to use for menu design and disc content. Give these ideas to the production team so that they can be added to the shooting script.

Design Navigation and Interaction

DVDs are too often considered an output medium like VHS. Clients assume once the DVD is put into the player everything is fine. This oversight, however, perpetuates two myths: whatever is put on the DVD will be usable, and DVDs offer simplistic interaction. DVD-Video is obviously more interactive than VHS because the viewer can skip through content quicker, can access additional information, and has control over the viewing experience.

This section guides you through designing DVD navigation and interaction. I explain working methods and the tools used to create navigation. I introduce principles of DVD interaction, and I cover the navigation found typically on DVDs while pointing out things you can do to make your projects easier to implement and easier to navigate.

Process

I liken navigation, interaction, and visual design to creating structure, form, and finish to the DVD. Navigation is akin to Web information architecture. It is the structural categorization of content that creates meaningful paths to information for viewers. Interaction design gives the experience form through controls and models that help in accessing and understanding content. Visual design is the application of communication and motion design principles to speak to, delight, and support the viewer. A project is most successful when navigation, interaction, and visual design are created within a close team supported by research.

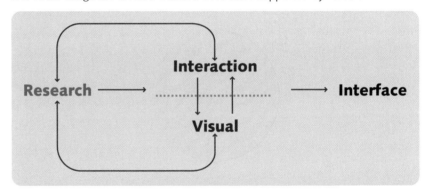

Figure 3-3: **Relationship between navigation, interaction, and visual design**

Interaction Design Deliverables

The two deliverables that document the navigation and interaction design are flowcharts and menu warerooms. These are similar to a Web site's site map and page schematics or warerooms.

Tools of the Trade

I have consistently used the following items to design DVDs, Web sites and software applications. They have been indispensable in the design process.

PENCIL AND PAPER

Getting excited over art materials reminds me of the hours I spent exploring a design school's art store. A high school English teacher told me Hemingway drew inspiration from sharpening pencils before writing. Well, I like soft number 2 Ticonderoga brand pencils; you know, the ones from the days of standardized tests. Coupled with a hearty plastic or rubber eraser, and you have nearly unlimited undos. Black felt pens are excellent for sketching because they photocopy and reproduce extremely well. For paper, I prefer bright white letter- and tabloid-size paper. I use letter-size for sketching wireframes and tabloid-size for flowcharts. Both photocopy extremely well, assuming you are using a copier that can copy tabloid-size originals.

To share ideas quickly scan your drawings, place them in a page layout application, and create a PDF. I scan the drawings at 150 to 300 dots per inch and run simple level adjustments to improve contrast. Although photocopies are sufficient for reviews with local clients, this technique works very well with remote clients and, team members, looks a bit more professional, and if everyone uses the commenting features in Acrobat, helps you review the designs.

 I have put an InDesign template that you can use to create these sketches. Use paper-sketches.indd in the Interaction Design folder.

WHITEBOARDS AND A DIGITAL CAMERA
Almost every workplace—whether it is a design firm or a tech company—has whiteboards in most rooms. Some rooms have whiteboards that cover the entire wall. The luxury of drawing with this much space can really liberate you. The downside is that someone can come in later and erase everything you have done, even if you have posted a save note.

Instead of taking a half hour to transcribe the design to paper, have a digital camera ready. The key in taking a photo of the sketch is to make sure that there is no glare on the white board and that you are getting all the details in the drawing. My advice is to take a photo and view it on the camera's LCD display. Zoom in to see if you are recording the white board properly. Take a few photos if you cannot capture it in one take—you can always stitch them together in Photoshop.

Flowcharts
A flowchart shows all the links between every menu and timeline on the disc, and because it is a bird's-eye view of the DVD, it is crucial to DVD production. For example, editors use the flowchart to create video segments, the menu designer uses it to produce designs for all the menus and menu transitions, authors use it to

create all the necessary links and behaviors, and quality assurance engineers use it to write test plans, validate links, and check transcode quality. In addition, a flowchart helps familiarize new team members with a project and helps them to compare, create, and plan new projects.

 Learning how to Learn *by Novak and Gowin is an excellent book if you are looking to improve your flow charting and diagraming skills.*

THE ELEMENTS OF A FLOWCHART

A flowchart usually contains the following elements: the first play item, menus, and timelines. The diagram also displays audio and subtitle track information and menu playback properties that indicate whether or not the a menus is timed, infinite, looped a number of times, or looped infinitely.

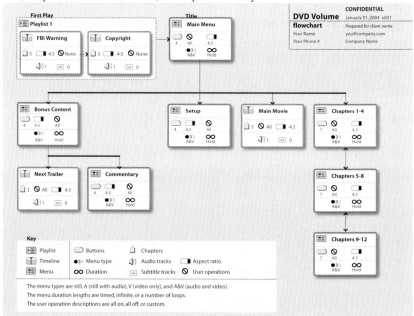

Figure 3-4: **DVD Flowchart elements**

All DVDs begin with a first play. As mentioned earlier, the first play is often the FBI warning video, or an introductory video, even the main menu. Because it is the first thing shown, it is placed prominently so people know where to begin examining the flow.

A flowchart does not need to show each button on a menu, but it should show the links created by the buttons. These links appear as one form of connection between menus and timelines. Likewise for timelines, it is often difficult to show every chapter point because a timeline has up to 99 chapter points.

CREATING A FLOWCHART FROM START TO FINISH

Developing a flowchart should begin soon after you understand the project's scope. I like to begin flowcharts early. When talking with the client, I will go up to a white board and roughly sketch a flow. As I draw the diagram, I talk through it, asking the client questions as needed. Because it is all on the whiteboard, it is easy to erase one idea and sketch a new idea quickly. When the session is done, I take a picture of the whiteboard with a digital camera. I have found that a 2-megapixel or larger resolution camera works best. Be careful to not catch too much glare, or parts of the whiteboard will be obscured. Also, write legibly and use markers that create solid lines. Post the photograph for discussion. Save it as a PDF if you want people to add comments directly to it.

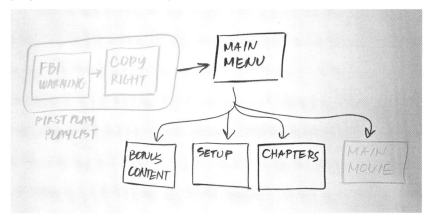

Figure 3-5: **Sample flowchart diagram**

Once you have the flowchart recorded, draw it in a program like Microsoft Visio or Adobe Illustrator. Having the flowchart in a digital form allows you to make frequent updates quickly, and you can reuse flowchart components again and again.

If you can, always sketch the initial flowchart. Although this sounds contradictory to the previous paragraph, a sketch is often faster to produce, it can be done anywhere and by anyone, and it is judged fairly because of its rough appearance.

The sample flowcharts are in Illustrator file format and include symbols for common flowchart items. It is located in the Interaction Design folder.

Create headers and footers in the flowchart. In the header, include the modification date, the version, the project name, and the author's name and e-mail for questions. In the footer, include a key and footnotes. Another handy device is a short naming scheme for menus and timelines. Although this process is entirely optional, it facilitates the creation of large projects with more than one author. Conventions such as these are even better when everyone on the team understands and uses the conventions.

DVD-ROM CONTENT

Encore DVD allows you to publish computer-readable files on a DVD by selecting a DVD-ROM folder (see *Disc Tab* on page 135 for more information). If you plan to publish HTML, PDF, or other computer files on the DVD, create a list of this content.

 If you publish a large number of HTML and PDF documents on the DVD, the ROM portion of the disc might be another project.

Wire Frames

As you develop the flowchart, you start to see all the menus and timelines that need to be created. For simple projects, a flowchart is sufficient. For large projects with many menus and timelines, wire frames help production in a few ways. It helps you prototype the disc quickly without having to shoot video, link up menus, and so on. And like a flowchart, wire frames help everyone on the team with their production tasks.

MENU WIREFRAMES

Menu wireframes detail all the content and interactive elements on a single menu. You should include the following items on a menu wire frame:

- The menu's name and a short descriptive name.

- A short description of the timeline.

- The menu buttons, and each button's Link and Override properties. If the menu has hidden buttons that link to "easter eggs," secret menus, or timelines, include these.

- The menu's timing and motion properties:

- Is it held forever or does it have a duration?

- Video or audio backgrounds. For instance the content in the menu, (e.g., "short clip of trolleys on California Street with conductor yelling, 'All aboard!'").

- The loop point and number of loops.

- Transitions that lead into or out of the menu.

- End Action and Override properties, if applicable.

- The default button.

- Button routing.

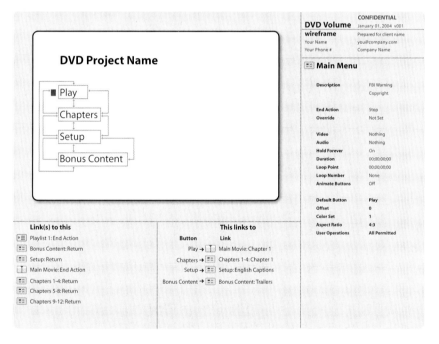

Figure 3-6: **Menu wire frame**

TIMELINE WIREFRAMES

Timeline wireframes should contain:

- The timeline's name.

- A short description of the timeline.

- The timeline chapters.

- The timeline's duration.

- The timeline's tracks.

  - Audio track content. The number of audio tracks and each track's content and language.

  - Subtitle track content. The number of subtitle tracks and each track's content and language.

- Remote Menu, End Action, and Override properties, if applicable.

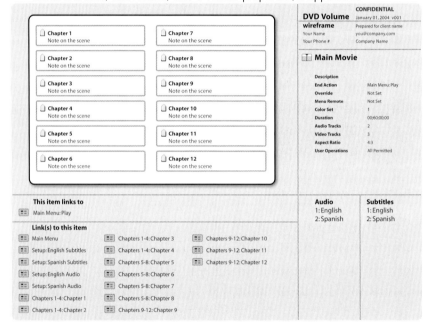

Figure 3-7: **Timeline wire frame**

PLAYLIST WIREFRAMES
Playlist wireframes should contain:

- The playlist's name.

- The timelines that are in the playlist.

- The playlist's End Action.

Figure 3-8: **Playlist Wireframe**

Helpful Questions

After conducting user research and watching the project's video, designing navigation and menu interaction is not always straightforward. When I have a hard time deciding what to design, I keep the viewer's needs in mind. I recall the user profiles and phrase questions in terms of what they need.

Flowchart Questions

- What is the most logical organization of the content? Does your project have one video segment? Are there ways to break it into logical chapters? If there will be more than one video, how many menus do you need to introduce to provide access to the video content?

- What does the viewer see after inserting the disc? This item is the first play. Every project should have one. It is usually the FBI warning, but in other cases, it could be the main menu, a company's logo animation, or a short video introducing the disc.

- What is on the main menu? Remember that you have a limit of 36 buttons and maybe fewer if you are designing for multiple aspect ratios. What can be on this menu versus what you can place on a secondary menu?

- What happens when the user clicks the remote control's Title button? The Title button is like a universal Home button on a Web site. The link for the Title button may not be the same item as for the first play, but it can be. Think of a Web site with an animated introduction that plays before showing the homepage. The animated introduction is shown first, but the homepage is the primary way to access the site. On a DVD, the first play is like the animated introduction, and the main menu is like the homepage.

Menu Questions

- On any menu, where is this most important button? Not only should this button be given additional prominence, but it should be the menu's default button. The default button is automatically selected when the menu is loaded.

- How much time should the user spend on this screen? Is the menu going to be a still menu and play forever until the user chooses a button, or will it time out and go somewhere else if no button is chosen?

- What links should be available at all times? In most cases, this should be the main menu, but if the project has many levels of menus, you need to provide buttons that go up a level as well as to the top level.

Timeline Interaction Design Questions

- Will the timeline have additional audio or subtitle tracks? Will you provide menus to select these additional tracks?

- Where will the timeline go after it plays? Will it go to another timeline, or will it return to the menu that played it?

Playlist Interaction Design Questions

- Is it desireable to construct multiple paths through the project? If it is, playlists can help construct these paths.

- Where will the playlist go after it plays? Will it go to a timeline, a menu, or another playlist?

Interaction Design Tips

The following design rules can help you put into practice your navigation and interaction. They are not complete, and some can be broken, but like the previous set questions, they can bring order and clarity to wayward designs.

- *Keep it simple.* Remember that often, less is more. A cluttered interface is hard to use, and given the limited screen real estate on televisions, you cannot provide links to everything. Perhaps the one saving grace of the DVD specification is that it is far simpler than HTML. That said, do not fashion the DVD interface as a Web site, and do not fall into the trap many poor Web designers fall into by overloading the screen with too much stuff.

- *Be consistent.*
    - Place buttons in the same place.
    - Create consistent routing between buttons across menus.
    - Keep selection and activation colors consistent across button groups.
    - Set remote control menu button links in the same way.
    - Use the same wording for buttons that have the same link.

- *Provide adequate feedback.* When a viewer selects a button, the visual state of the button should be unique from the other buttons. Treat selected buttons and nonselected buttons consistently.

- *Use simple language that viewers understand.* Do not succumb to irony and use clever wording that the viewer will not understand. For specialized projects, do research and ask participants what terminology and wording is understood in their community of interest.

- *Provide links to the main menu on every menu.* If the menu is a child menu under another menu, provide a link to the parent menu. For menus that are several layers deep, provide links to the main menu and the menu above the current menu.

- *Create logical chapter points in timelines and create chapter menus.* This gives the viewer the ability to continue when they are not able to watch the entire DVD in one session. If there are logical chapters in the video content, set them at the same interval and include the time interval on the chapter selection menu.

- *Provide help.* This can be a video or a short printed instructional booklet. If you cannot afford to print an insert to go with the disc, place a short video or still menu at the beginning of the disc explaining that there is an instructional file on the DVD-ROM portion of the disc.

Prototyping

Prototyping is creating a functional version of the project for evaluation purposes. The goal is to gain valuable feedback on the project's features before production. When prototyping a DVD project, you have the following options.

- Create a paper prototype from sketches, wireframes, or Photoshop files.
- Author a small subset of the project and build a DVD folder or disc.

PAPER PROTOTYPING

This option can be produced in a few hours. Usually you want to test to see whether people get the idea and purpose of the project, test your naming scheme, and test overall functionality. You can create prototypes at any stage of development, but prototyping with paper at the beginning has the most bang for the buck because paper prototypes are produced quickly and cheaply and yield a lot of valuable feedback. There is no need to make huge investments in production and design when an hour's worth of sketching and a few interviews will do.

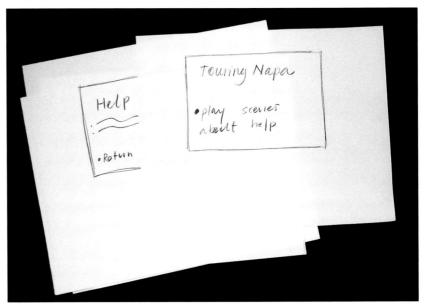

Figure 3-9: **Paper prototype**

You can use either hand-drawn sketches or the wireframes for paper prototypes. I usually conduct two to three rounds of quick testing with paper sketches before moving to the more finished wireframes. If there is time, I will do two to three rounds of testing with more finished wireframes before beginning production.

Authoring a Functionally Limited DVD

Putting four to five menus with video on a disc is easy to do given Encore DVD's simplified link creation tools. Determining what and how much video content to show should be determined early. If you include video for the sake of feedback on the presentation and content of the video, include as much as you need. If you are only testing menu design and navigation, include a small amount that makes moving between menus and video possible.

When you author a small test, your options are to burn the project to disc, build a DVD image, or build a DVD folder. A disc is flexible because it plays on both DVD players and computers. DVD players are cheap and easy to carry and connect to almost any television manufactured in the last several years. Using a DVD player is also important if the project is meant to be viewed on one. Viewing the prototype on a computer is more a matter of convenience. A DVD image or folder can only be guaranteed to play on a computer; not all DVD software players can play them. The advantage of the image or folder is that you save the expense and time of burning a disc.

When testing a functionally limited DVD, you test for the same things—does the viewer get the idea and purpose? More importantly, with the benefit of designing a few screens, you are testing whether the visual design makes interacting with the disc easy.

Usability Testing

Usability should not be left until the end because it is, hands down, the best method for discovering potential interface problems. Ideally it begins as up-front research and continues throughout production with testing. By testing iteratively, you learn from the viewers what makes the project easy to use and enjoyable. The usability testing process involves the following steps.

1. *Planning.* Write the screening questionnaire used in recruiting and the test plan, which covers the goals and content of the usability tests.
2. *Recruiting.* Contact or find test participants who match the audience criteria.

3. *Testing.* Run tests and make note of usability issues and opportunities to improve interaction.

4. *Analyzing test results.* Examine and report test results and make recommendations for improvements.

Planning and Recruiting

Remember when I talked about conducting viewer research at the onset of a project? At that time, I described locating people who fit the audience's criteria for interviews. In some cases, you can test the people you interviewed because they are prequalified. The screening techniques used to locate these people are also used to locate people for usability testing. You rely on the user profiles that the screener originally created, and possibly updated after research to locate test participants.

WRITING THE TEST PLAN

The test plan is the framework written before testing begins. It is often a collaboration between the usability researcher, the designer, and a project manager. It is usually organized into the following sections:

- What are the test objectives? What areas will be tested, and how long will it take to complete tasks?

- Who is the audience for the tests? How many people need to be tested? Who are the test participants and what are their backgrounds?

- What will be the testing methodology? Will paper prototypes or a test build be used? Will it be recorded? Will the participant be asked to use the "talk aloud" principle, or will the session be an interview?

- When and where will the tests take place? What computer, audio, and video resources need to be acquired for the testing?

- What is the budget for testing? Include a breakdown for participant remuneration, facilitator salaries, and facility rental.

 The test plan can benefit quality assurance teams because they can model their quality assurance plans on the same criteria.

Testing

If you are testing several people at one location, give each participant clear instructions to the test location, and have someone ready to greet and lead them to the waiting area before the test. Provide a few magazines, a glass of water, and a comfortable chair. While participants wait for their turn, it is a good time to have them sign consent forms and confidentiality agreements. Have phone numbers for each participant handy, and give them a courtesy call a day before to remind them about the time of their appointment and the location.

 Renting research labs is not cheap. Have a few backup participants available to replace scheduled participants who fail to show or who cancel.

The procedure for nearly all usability tests begins by giving the user an orientation, a prequestionnaire, and a list of tasks, and ends with a postquestionnaire. A facilitator runs the test, and another person might be needed to take notes, to help with technical snafus, or to play the part of DVD player if paper prototypes are used.

ORIENTATION

In the orientation, the facilitator begins with introductions and tells the participant what she will be evaluating. It is important to stress that the product is being tested and that the product development team is looking for her candid and honest opinion. When I have run tests as an independent consultant, I tell the participant that I am not with the company and that she should feel free to tell me whatever she likes because I will not be offended. Tell the participant that the prototype is limited and does not do everything the final product will do. Continue by saying that you will point out when there are areas that are not fully functional.

 A sample orientation script along with sample questionnaires and task lists are included in the Usability folder..

PREQUESTIONNAIRE

A prequestionaire can help verify information collected during the test screening, and it is a good place to collect additional information before the test begins and the participants have been exposed to the product. You can let them fill the form out, or you can ask the questions and fill the form out yourself. I tend to let them fill out the form, and after the test, I look for incomplete entries and ask for missing information.

TASK LIST

The task list is the set of tasks the participant will perform during the session. It should be no more than two pages, broken down by each screen shown in the test, and you should provide the participant with a scenario that frames a use of the DVD.

Before handing over the list, the facilitator needs to communicate that the participant need not complete all the tasks, that the facilitator cannot help with completing the tasks, and what the test protocol is—talk aloud, observation, or interview.

If the participant feels uncomfortable, tired, or wants to take a break, it is acceptable to stop the test. Ask the participant whether he needs a break or wants to stop the session. If he wants to stop, thank him for his time before he leaves.

If the participant does not understand a task, it is okay to explain it, but do not explain how to complete it. When the participant asks for help completing a task, say, "I am not allowed to help," and offer as much encouragement as possible.

 You should never lead or help the viewer through the test because this defeats the purpose of objectively testing for usability.

For example, if a viewer was on a chapter selection menu and did not know that clicking a button labeled Back took them to the main menu, the facilitator should ask things like, "Where will the Back button go to?" If the viewer did not see the Back button, the facilitator might ask, "What links to the main menu?" Remember to always phrase questions that are open. Do not place judgement on the design, and do not make the viewer feel as if he is being tested.

Test methodologies include talk aloud (the most effective), observation, and interview. When following the talk aloud principle, the participant says out loud what he is thinking as he interacts with the prototype. He should say what he reads or sees, what assumptions and expectations he has about the interface, and how he feels about the interface as he experiences it. Tell the person that likes and dislikes are equally appreciated, and ask him not to hold back. If you use this method, tell the participant that you will ask him to speak up or to continue talking if he becomes silent. If the participant does not understand how to do this, give him an example. I usually say, "I am putting the DVD into the player. I see some text with the FBI warning on it. I guess I cannot copy this DVD for my own commercial use. Now I see the production company's logo. I like it. This is transitioning into a menu with the name of the movie across the top and five links on the menu, they are..."

With the observation method, the participant simply performs the tasks and the facilitator takes notes. The interview method will have more interaction between the participant and facilitator as the participant attempts and performs each task to completion. Personally, I like to mix talk aloud with some interview, but I encourage the participant to talk as much as possible.

If you are running a test in which there is a separate observation lounge, please tell any team members in the lounge to remain quiet during the test. It can make participants feel uncomfortable if they know there are other people watching and commenting on their decisions. One unfortunate but funny incident occurred when I was testing the Shutterfly Web site in New York. The homepage text contained the words "click here," and unfortunately the spacing between the c and l was too tight. When the participant read the text aloud, she was not only confused, but a little offended. It was very hard to suppress the laughter that came from the observation lounge during that test!

 If team members are observing you on video or from behind a two-way mirror, use hand signals to quiet them down.

OBSERVATION TIPS

During the test, you should play close attention to the interaction between the participant and the prototype. If it turns out that you cannot take notes and facilitate at the same time, your options are to tape the session and take notes later or to have a few people in an observation room taking notes for you. When observing users, note the following.

- Does the user complete each task successfully? What tasks are easy and which ones are hard? Note the time taken to complete each task.

- What is the participant saying at any given moment? Is the user confident, happy, frustrated, or confused?

- When and how frequently does the participant look for help or give up?

- Does the participant tell you about similar experiences with other DVDs, Web sites, or other products? Does she say she really likes the other approach or does she say the prototype has done a better job?

When interviewing, remember the advice given in *Keep the Discussion Open* on page 42—do not pass judgement and keep things open-ended.

POSTTEST QUESTIONNAIRE AND DEBRIEFING

After the tasks are complete or time is becoming short, tell the participant that time is running out, you would like him to answer a few questions about his experience, and you would like him to rate the product overall for ease of use and enjoyment.

This questionnaire should provide both a scale on which to rate answers and space to enter comments. The ranking provides you with data for compilation and statistical analysis. The free-form comments are more qualitative and provide good sound bites for the report. Again, if the user completes the questionnaire himself, remember to look it over quickly; if he has left questions unanswered, ask him to answer these questions before leaving.

After the participant leaves, I collect the questionnaire and make sure the participant's name is on all the forms and place them together. After all the sessions are complete, I photocopy my notes and organize them with the questionnaires. This makes writing the report much faster!

TESTING PAPER PROTOTYPES

When you test a paper prototype, it is best to have two people run the test with viewers. One person facilitates, and the second person plays the part of the DVD player. If you are the facilitator, introduce yourself and your colleague playing the role of the DVD player and explain your roles. The facilitator orients the viewer and leads the session. The DVD player shows and hides screens as the user "clicks" buttons.

The person playing the part of the DVD player should be very organized! Keep all the paper prototypes in order and be familiar with the test script. Often the designer or the DVD authoring engineer should play the role of the DVD player while someone else facilitates. The DVD player should not help the viewer and should never take screens away before the viewer is done. The person in this role needs to be patient and should not talk with the viewer. If the viewer asks the player a question, that person should say (with some bit of humor), "I am only the DVD player, I cannot answer any questions."

After the introductions, the facilitator begins the test by saying the viewer has hypothetically inserted the disc into the player; the person acting as the player begins to show the user the paper prototype and the viewer begins trying to complete the list of tasks.

EVALUATING TEST BUILDS

At the beginning of the session, hand the disc to the participant with the task list and have her insert the disc into the player. Remind her to be patient with the prototype since it is not fully functional and has a few rough spots. As with the paper prototype test, do not coach the participant. Only offer assistance when the participant accesses an area that is not functional or is not part of the test.

If you are using a DVD player, make sure there are fresh batteries in the remote. Place the DVD player so that there is a clear line of sight between the player and the remote. As with software or Web site testing, be sure to run through the test before the sessions in case you need to fix missing elements that are crucial to the test.

Analyzing Test Results

Write the report when the sessions are still fresh in your mind. You can forget a lot of useful information if you wait too long after the test. Although you can always watch the video tapes of the sessions, you probably won't unless you are going to include segments of them in your usability presentation or you are bursting to watch them.

ASSESSING THE RESULTS

When observing and reporting usability issues, consider how frequently something occurs in a test, and whether it is credible given the areas that are being tested, the users being tested, and the quality of the prototype. For instance, if every participant does not understand the wording of a button, most likely the wording should be changed. On the other hand, someone who is not part of the target audience and is not familiar with the subject matter does not understand or approve of the wording although other participants do, you should discount the opinion of the outside participant. Also, if participants become hung up on an area that is not fully fleshed out or is not part of the areas being tested, be ready to discount those findings too.

WRITING THE USABILITY REPORT

The usability report needs to summarize the test results, recommend design and functional changes, and then list the detailed findings from the test sessions. A report should have a table of contents with the following sections: introduction, summary, list of recommendations, and detailed findings.

 A sample report template is located on the DVD in the Usability folder.

When summarizing the test, briefly describe the area of the project tested and who evaluated it. List the usability problems that occur most frequently and give an explanation of how the problem occurs and what occurs after the problem. Quotes from the participants can help stress the importance of specific usability issues. Use charts only when they show important trends or comparisons. Do not sugarcoat problems, and do not be completely negative. Write a fair assessment that recognizes strengths and weaknesses. The purpose of testing is to make the product better; it is not to pat the development team on the back or tell them they are doing a less than perfect job. If you do too much of either, they will not need or want to hire you again.

In making recommendations, correlate recommendations to usability issues and explain why they will address the issue. Identify what changes will make the biggest difference in overall usability. Also rate each recommendation on how expensive it is. Will it require a lot of work to be redone or is it a small change (e.g., a different link or word change)? Narrow the list to 10 major recommendations and then follow with the rest.

The detailed findings can be as long and as raw as you want to make them. Most people who review a report sadly read only the summary and recommendations. For a basic report, you can simply transcribe your notes and place the questionnaire answers after each subject heading. If you have more time, you can create a table that shows each task and the responses from several participants, or you can organize the findings into these areas: navigation, functionality, feedback, language, and consistency.

Design

In addition to interaction design, designing menus draws on several skill sets rooted in fine and applied art: typography, color, and image making.

This chapter presents the following topics:

- Graphic design principles
- Combining type and images
- Production tips

Graphic Design Principles

Graphic design communicates information visually. Successful design does this in a way that is functional, appropriate, consistent, crafted, and delightful.

- *Function.* Is the design functional? For instance, can people read it and do they understand what elements are interactive? Does it solve a problem?

- *Appropriateness.* Appropriate design speaks to an the audience effectively. It can share sentiment with the audience, create a sense of ease, or compel the audience to act. Appropriate design is not ignored.

- *Consistency.* Is the type set the same way? Are the buttons positioned in the same way? Inconsistency creates jarring experiences for viewers. The result can be confusion, irritation, or dissatisfaction.

- *Craft.* Good craft shows attention to detail, careful execution, consistency, high production value, and a fresh understanding of design principles.

- *Delight.* Design that delights satisfies the viewers for any number of reasons. It is a measurement of the overall quality of the experience. Delight can occur when the viewer finds humor or surprise in the design.

Successful design follows a *process* and develops *visual language*. The process is informed and guided by research. The visual language is a system for typography, color, imagery, and animation.The system is developed through sketches, color studies, storyboards, and animatics. The sketches explore strategies for creating hierarchy, contrast, and style.

Typography

Typography is the practice of arranging text for communication. If the text does not communicate, it is not typography, although it might be fine art or illustration. Typographic principles have been in place for centuries, but only within the past 20 years can typography be done by anyone with a personal computer. As powerful as these tools are, they do not guarantee clear communication, and a lot of bad design results because the tools are so accessible. Like many craft-oriented professions, typography has to be learned and practiced, so it is important that those lacking a design education learn typographic principles.

Parts of a Typeface

Figure 4-1: **The tool is responsible for the form**

To understand the graphic form of type requires a look at the development of Roman, or Western, letter forms. As letter forms progressed from stone tablet to paper, the tools used to create them influenced their form and are the reason we have serif and italic typefaces and a number of display typefaces based on historical letter forms. The brush is the reason we have serifs, and the quill and nibbed pen are responsible for italics.

As movable type was invented, the forms were modified to suit printing. In 1471, Nicolas Jenson developed a single type family in which the uppercase from the Romans, namely the Trajan column, was combined with the uncial, or lowercase, letter forms from Carolingian miniscule. His letter forms were far more even in tone, and the combination of both cases improved legibility substantially.

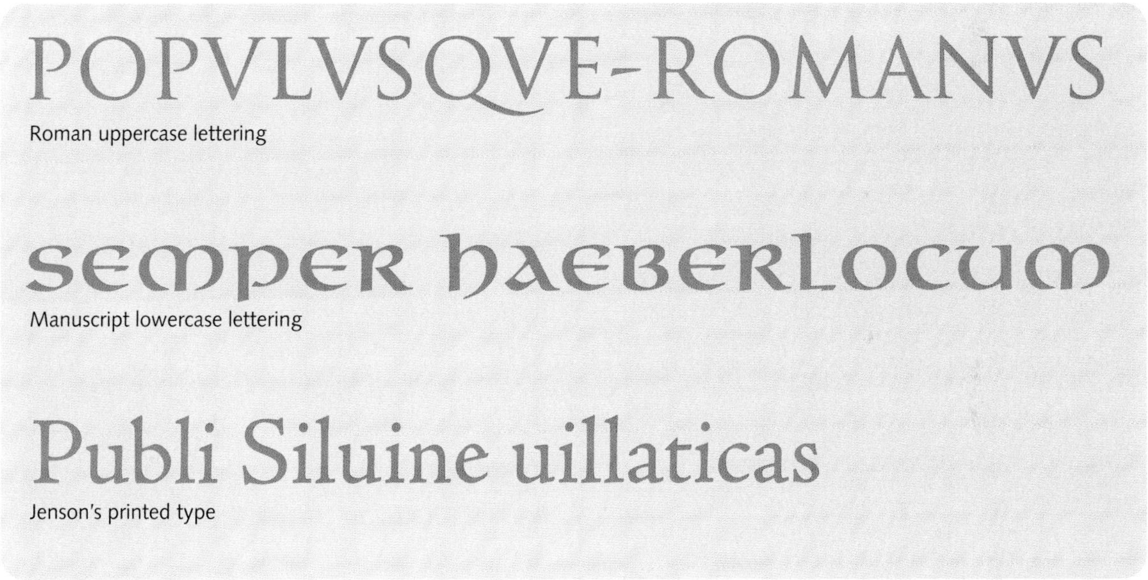

POPVLVSQVE-ROMANVS
Roman uppercase lettering

SEMPER HAEBERLOCUM
Manuscript lowercase lettering

Publi Siluine uillaticas
Jenson's printed type

Figure 4-2: **The development of the modern alphabet of upper- and lowercase letters**

Although the graphic style of type has continuously been revised, the basic forms in Jenson's typeface are fairly close to today's serif typefaces. This is a testament to how radically different his design was from those of his contemporaries and how successful his contribution to typography has been.

Indentifying type is a useful skill when working with corporate design standards, choosing and purchasing type, and validating typographic consistency. Knowing the anatomical forms of type and the representation of these forms across varying typefaces helps indentify type.

To sharpen your indentification skills, quiz yourself on the typefaces you see. What is the name, who created it, and how is it classified?

THE PARTS

Given the number of upper- and lowercase letters in typeface and the variations of typefaces that exist, many distinct parts create letter forms and unity within a typeface design (Figure 4-3).

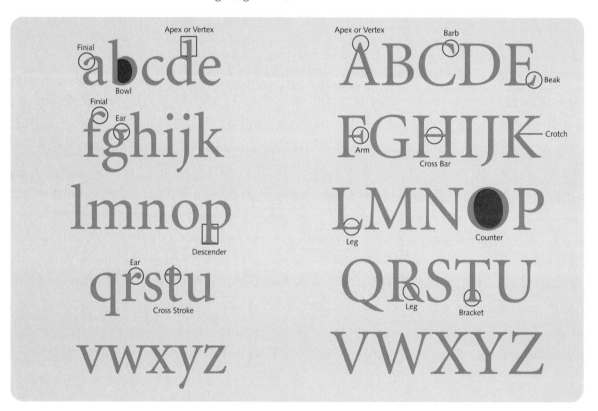

Figure 4-3: **The parts of letter forms**

VERTICAL PROPORTIONS

Almost all typefaces have a baseline, a median, an x-height, a cap height, an ascender height, and a descender height. These are all invisible guides that run horizontally and measure a typeface's vertical proportions. Type rests upon the baseline. The median is the top boundary of most lowercase characters (e.g., a, c, e, g, etc.). The space between the baseline and the median is the x-height, which

as its name implies, is the height of the lowercase x. Cap height is the distance
between the baseline and the top of the uppercase. Ascender height is the space
between the baseline and the top boundary of lowercase characters that ascend
above the median (e.g., b,d,f,h,k,l). Descender height is the extent to which lowercase letter forms extend below the baseline (e.g., g,j,p,q,y).

Figure 4-4: **Vertical proportions**

Font Classification

Type families are classified by their graphic form and by their place in history. The
major categories are serif, sans serif, and display. Each category has subcategories
that classify type further.

SERIF

Serif type has its roots in the type that was carved in stone and drawn with an
angled pen and brush. The serif is the product of the writing instrument completing a vertical or diagonal stroke. For 500 years, typeface designers have continued

to vary strokes and serifs to create new typefaces. Today, serif typefaces are classified as Old Style, Transitional, Modern, or Slab Serif.

Old Style Serif typefaces

Transitional Serif typefaces

Modern Serif typefaces

Slab Serif **Serif typefaces**

Figure 4-5: **The serif**

As mentioned earlier, Old Style typefaces were developed during the Renaissance in Italy and combined classical Roman uppercase and Carolingian lowercase. Centaur, a revival design by Bruce Rogers, and Bembo, designed by Francesco Griffo, are examples of Old Style from this period. In France, two notable Old Style typefaces were developed: Garamond and Granjon. Caslon, the last of the original Old Style typefaces, was developed in early 17th century England. Because Old Style type is derivative from written letter forms, it has bracketed asymmetrical serifs and a diagonal stress that creates contrast between horizontal and vertical strokes.

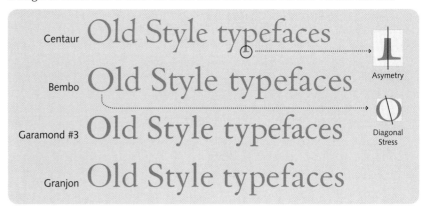

Figure 4-6: **Old Style typefaces**

Transitional typefaces lie between the hand-drawn quality of Old Style and the severe contrast of Modern typefaces. They were created because printing technology improved and made thinner serifs possible. In addition, the influence of handwritten letter forms decreased. Baskerville and Caslon are good examples of Transitional type. Transitional type has significantly less diagonal stress, and the serifs are more, but not perfectly, symmetrical.

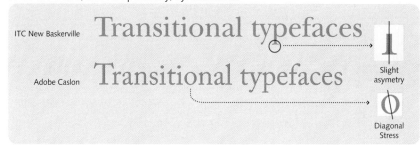

Figure 4-7: **Transitional typefaces**

Modern typefaces do not refer to type developed in the current day. Instead, they refer to type developed during significant printing advances in the late 18th century. Modern typefaces such as Bodoni are completely devoid of any reference to handwritten letter forms. The stress is perfectly perpendicular to the baseline. Modern is also referred to as Didot.

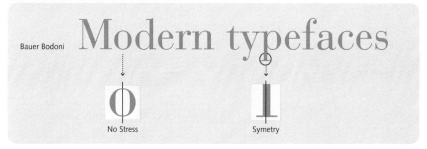

Figure 4-8: **Modern typefaces**

Slab Serif, or Egyption, typefaces were created in the late 18th century and were created for display purposes. Many people were critical of the design because Slab Serifs have less variation between stroke and serif and because the serifs are very thick slabs, hence the name Slab Serif. Although classifying these typefaces as Egyptian seems inappropriate, at the time, Egyptian antiquities were hip, and these type styles were promoted as being ancient, or Egyptian. Sometimes it is all about the marketing! Clarendon and Cheltenham are two fine examples of Slab Serif type.

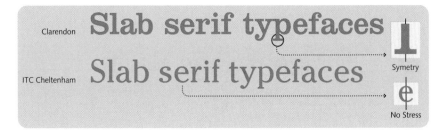

Figure 4-9: **Slab Serif typefaces**

 The best way to classify serif type is by the shape of the serif and by the amount of diagonal stress characters have from the y-axis.

SANS SERIF

In the early 19th century, sans serif typefaces were developed to mimic the lettering style seen in sign painting. Initially, sans serif type was available only in large sizes—Poster or wood type are excellent examples of early sans serif type—and was classified as Lineal, Humanist, and Geometric.

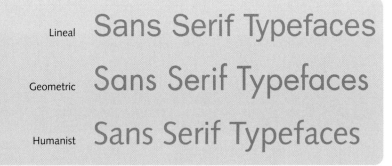

Figure 4-10: **Sans Serif typefaces**

Lineal or ATypI, a term created by the international typography organization, depicts the early sans serif typefaces. I will refer to them as ATypI. These early sans serif types were called Antique, Gothic, Egyptian, and Grotesque. Some of the printers at the time thought the absence of serifs conjured ancient letter forms of Egypt and Greece. While they correctly related the design to antiquity, the terms have always caused confusion because Slab Serif type is also called Egyptian and because Gothic also refers to German black letter type. Another group of printers referred to the type as Grotesque because they thought the typefaces were less refined than serif types. Franklin Gothic, Monotype Grotesque, News Gothic, and Helvetica are examples.

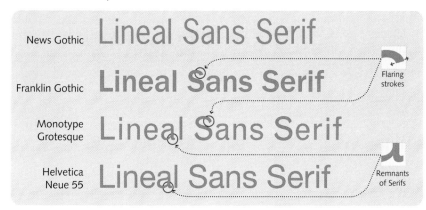

Figure 4-11: **Lineal sans serif typefaces**

Early 20th century modernism brought the Geometric class of sans serif type. This style was heavily influenced by the industrial and machine aesthetic started by the Bauhaus art school in Germany. Geometric typefaces are symmetrical and are constructed from straight lines and circles. Futura, designed by Paul Renner, is the most popular Geometric typeface, and Avenir and Avante Garde are two other examples.

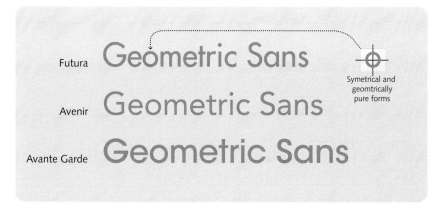

Figure 4-12: **Geometric sans serif typefaces**

Humanist sans serif faces were a response to Geometric sans serif typefaces. Rather than base the letter forms on geometry, Humanist type alludes to carved and handwritten letter forms. Humanist faces have proportions and a slight diagonal stress that are reminiscent of Old Style serif faces. Gill Sans was the first true Humanist typeface and Syntax, which this book uses, and Optima are examples.

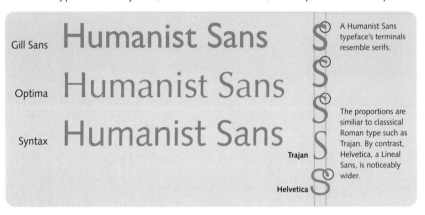

Figure 4-13: **Humanist Sans serif typefaces**

 The best way to classify sans serif type is by the amount of diagonal stress characters have from the y-axis, how uniform the strokes are, and how the strokes end.

BEYOND SANS AND SERIF TYPE

Black letter, monospaced, script, and display type are the other generalized type classifications. Black letter originated in Northern Europe and spread to France and England where it was quickly replaced with Old Style serif type. Black letter remained popular in Germany until the mid-20th century.

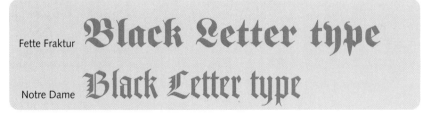

Figure 4-14: **Black letter typeface**

Variable-spaced type has variable widths for each letter form. For instance, the lowercase "i" takes up less space than the lowercase "m". The majority of typefaces are variable width. Monospaced type has a fixed width for all letter forms and was developed for typewriters.

Courier **Fixed width**   width

Prestige Elite **Fixed width**   width

Letterforms are compressed or stretched in fixed width typefaces. Compare this to the variable width typeface, Minion, below.

Figure 4-15: **Variable- and monospaced typefaces**

SCRIPT

Script lettering styles developed in 17th century England. The master calligraphers took the italic lettering styles from Italy and made them more cursive by keeping the pen on the page and by using large, round strokes.

Künstler Script *Wedding Day*

Snell Roundhand *Wedding Day*

Nuptial Script *Wedding Day*

Voluta Script *Wedding Day*

Figure 4-16: **Script lettering examples**

DISPLAY

Display is a catchall for all typefaces that are meant to be rendered at sizes larger than 14 points or pixels. Another kind of display type is poster type. Poster type is bold, very decorative, and not always easily classifiable as serif or sans serif because it is so ornate.

Display type was originally created for posters and advertisements, therefore you might hear display type referred to as poster type. Display typefaces can be based on classical roman letter forms, or they can take on entirely new shapes and forms.

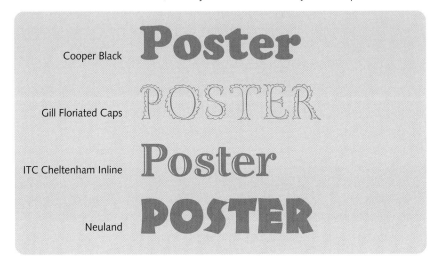

Figure 4-17: **A variety of Poster typefaces**

 Display and Script types should be set above 14 pixels because they often have delicate and intricate forms that reproduce poorly at small sizes.

In addition, serif typefaces often have display versions. These tend to be proportionally the same as body text, except thinner and more severe looking. These display typefaces are used in headlines, titles, and mastheads.

Display type is designed for headlines and large print. Since the letterforms are meant for large print, the strokes have a higher contrast between thick and thin.

Figure 4-18: **Display typefaces**

Typeface Families and Styles

A typeface family is a collection of styles that are similar in design and are meant to work together as a system when used for a book, signage system, or menu design. For instance, this book uses Syntax Roman for the body text, Syntax Bold for captions, and Syntax Black for the page number.

Both serif and sans serif typefaces often have additional type styles. The most common styles are roman, the normal typeface used for large passages of type; italic, the slanted or cursive version used for emphasis; and bold, the thicker version of the roman also used for emphasis and headlines. Although roman and italic designs are exclusive of one another, both roman and italic can have bold weights.

Also keep in mind that italics come in two forms. True italics is a separate design from the roman and follows the characteristics of cursive handwriting. Obliques are a version of the roman in which the type is slanted 10 to 15 degrees.

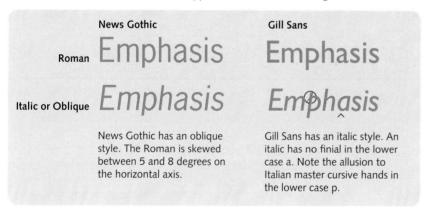

News Gothic

Roman   Emphasis

Italic or Oblique   Emphasis

News Gothic has an oblique style. The Roman is skewed between 5 and 8 degrees on the horizontal axis.

Gill Sans

Emphasis

Emphasis

Gill Sans has an italic style. An italic has no finial in the lower case a. Note the allusion to Italian master cursive hands in the lower case p.

Figure 4-19: **Italic and oblique typefaces**

CASE

Most typefaces have upper- and lowercase forms in a single style, but some typeface styles are only uppercase. Small capitals is a style in which both lowercase and uppercase letter sets have uppercase letter forms, but the lowercase letters comprise "smaller" capitals that are drawn at the x-height of the typeface. However, the smaller capitals are not merely a proportional reduction in size—they are drawn so that optically, they have the same weight or density as the uppercase form.

Real **SMALL CAPS** are

Fake **SMALL CAPS** are

Real small caps are drawn so their weight matches the weight of the tall caps.

When a computer fakes small capitals, the normal captials are scaled. Their weight does not match the tall caps and lower case. This creates an ugly and uneven effect.

Figure 4-20: **Small capitals**

Although digital typography can fake small capitals, in my opinion, they look worse than true small capitals.

WEIGHT AND WIDTH

Weight refers to the thickness of a type style's stroke. Common weight styles are light, regular, bold, and heavy. Typefaces with many weight styles will have extra light or ultralight, as well as extra heavy or ultraheavy. Light is also called thin. Thicker styles can be referred to as extra bold, heavy, or black.

Width refers to the proportion of x-axis relative to the y-axis. Weight styles vary from condensed to normal width to expanded width. Condensed is also called nar-

row or compressed. Additional names for expanded are wide and extended. These
two style variations can also be combined (Figure 4-21).

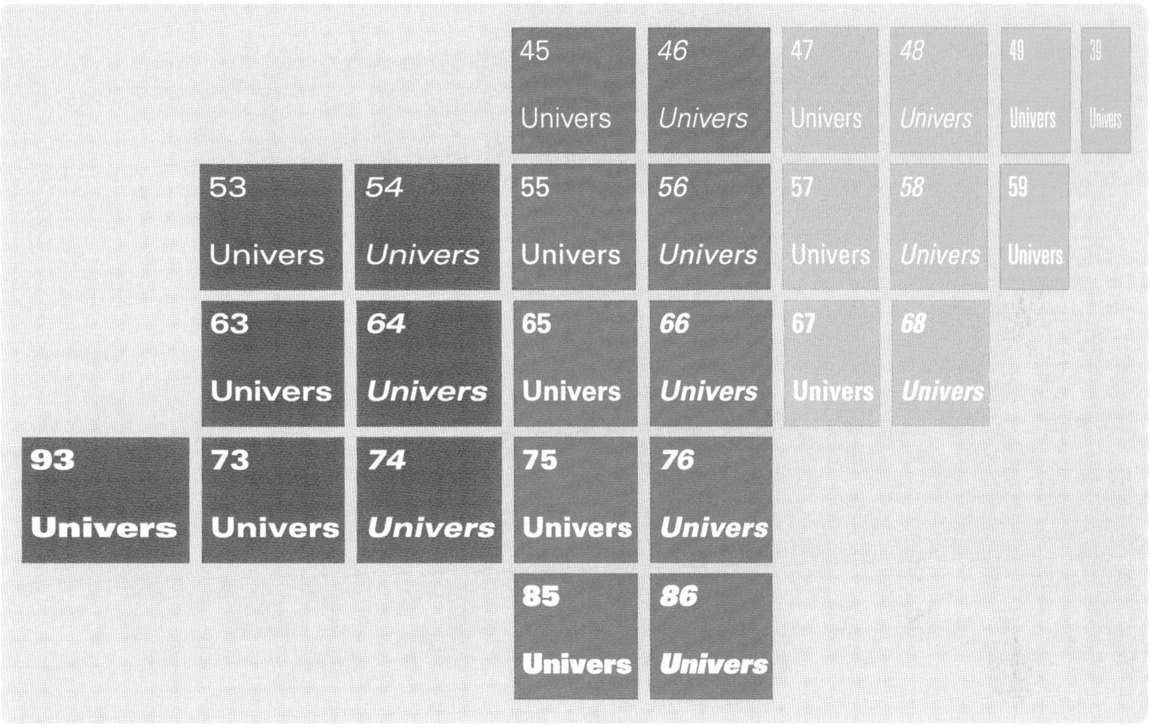

Figure 4-21: **Type style weight and width example**

Normally, setting body text in roman is recommended because it is most legible for
long passages of text. Menus, however, do not contain long passages of text, and
the text size on menus is larger than the size seen in the bodies of books and news-
papers. So menu design presents more flexibility in the type styles you can choose
than for headlines and body text.

Additional Styles in Typeface Families

Large typeface families have several, if not dozens of styles. In addition to styles
previously mentioned, there are: old style figures, display, ligatures, swash characters, alternates, dingbats, and optical variations. If you are looking for more information on the typefaces that come with Encore DVD, see *Type Included with
Encore DVD* on page 92.

NUMBERS

Numbers come in lining and nonlining varieties. Lining figures all rest on the baseline, are the same height, and are available in almost any typeface. Old-style numbers vary in height and vertical position relative to the baseline. Some numbers rest on the baseline, on the descender line, or on the baseline but rise to the ascender line.

Lining figures are best used when setting numbers with text set in all capitals, while old-style numbers are more legible in text passages. Old-style numbers are a separate style found in serif typeface, although they are built into a few OpenType serif families. Old-style numbers are best for setting numbers in text passages, but can add distinction when used for page numbers or in headings.

Either style of numbering can have tabular or proportional spacing. Tabular spacing is used for setting numbers that need to line up for ledgers and financial tables. Proportional numbers are used when setting numbers in passages of text.

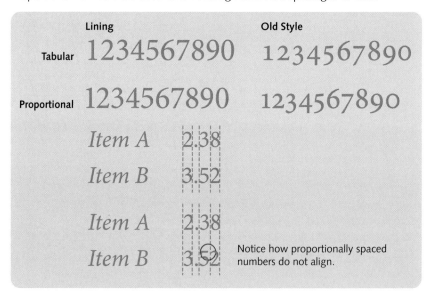

Figure 4-22: **Numbering styles**

If you want the weight of the numbers to appears less heavy and you want a more even texture, using a slightly smaller type size can help lining numbers look better in a paragraph of text.

Several OpenType typefaces with the "Pro" designation have professional typographic features built in. One of these features is advanced control over how numbers are set. You choose a style using the fly out menu in Photoshop's Character
palette. These numbering controls are exposed in Encore DVD's Character palette,
but Encore DVD will render the text properly.

*Use Photoshop for setting
more sophisticated text and
use Encore DVD for the basics.*

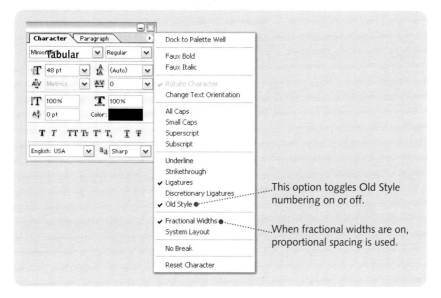

...This option toggles Old Style
numbering on or off.

When fractional widths are on,
proportional spacing is used.

Figure 4-23: **Photoshop's Character Palette and Opentype Features**

 *Serif typefaces often have nonlining character styles, while it is rarer that a
sans serif typeface has a nonlining style.*

LIGATURES, SWASH CHARACTERS, AND ALTERNATES

Ligatures are two characters that connect or are spaced so closely together that
they form a single character on a keyboard. Ligatures were originally created to
compensate for awkward spacing between two letter forms. Ligatures have also
been designed for decorative purposes. Swash characters and alternates are decorative alternatives for existing letter forms. Swash characters are mostly capital letters that start off a sentence or paragraph. Swash characters compliment text set in
italics. Alternates are mostly designed for specific placement. Some alternates

should only be used at the end or beginning of a line, but other alternates can be used inside text.

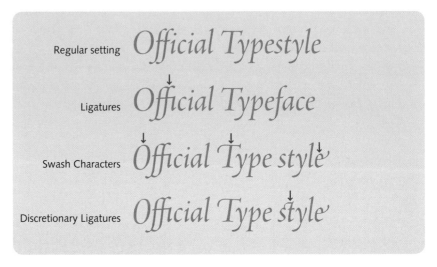

Figure 4-24: **Ligatures and swash characters**

DINGBATS

Dingbats, fleurons, and borders are symbols, decorative characters, and edge treatments. Dingbats can be used as informative symbols, such as bullets to punctuate a list of items, or as decorative marks, to end a story or article, for example. Fleurons are used as decorative marks in title pages, menus, and centered typography. Braces are the decorative edge treatments you often see on title pages or surrounding a small advertisement. They are created by placing eight different characters of a typeface, one for each corner and one for each side around the edges.

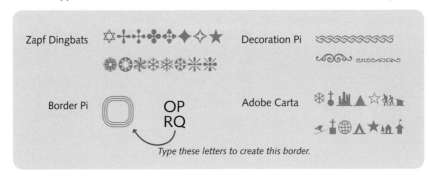

Figure 4-25: **Dingbat examples**

OPTICAL VARIATIONS

Optical variations were created for newspaper and book printing to reproduce text better at small sizes and to make text more compelling at large sizes. Some typefaces have designs for captions, small body text, and headlines. These designs vary the weight of the strokes and some do little tricks at the joins of strokes to "capture" more light. In Figure 4-26, three styles of Warnock Pro are shown. The display style has thinner cross strokes and should be set in a large size. The regular style is meant for body text. The caption style is subtly bolder and has a more even weight between vertical and horizontal strokes—these design elements make it easier to read at the smaller sizes.

Warnock Pro Display   ABCDEFGabcdefg

Warnock Pro Regular   ABCDEFGabcdefg

Warnock Pro Caption   ABCDEFGabcdefg

Figure 4-26: **Optical variations**

Punctuation and Typographic Marks

Proper punctuation and typographic marks show professionalism and craft. They also communicate and look better than the "one size fits all" marks provided on the keyboard. The two most common mistakes are not setting quotation marks properly and using a hyphen to interject a clause or show a range.

The main thing to remember is that each mark communicates specific information.

HYPHENS AND EM AND EN DASHES

Hyphens should only be used for hyphenation and compound words. Em dashes are used for interjection—like this. An en dash is a slightly narrower mark for separating two numbers in a range (e.g., 2002–2003), hyphenating open compounds (e.g., chapter index–style menu), or comparing words of equal weight (e.g., left–right alignment).

Parc is Xerox's research facility in Palo Alto, California, where the precursor to the Macintosh and Windows GUIs was developed—the Alto.

QUOTATION, TICK, AND INCH MARKS

Tick marks are what most people think of as a proper apostrophe and quotation marks. This could not be further from the truth! These two characters that share the same key and sit to the left of the Enter key are a remnant from the days when PCs hard dark caves for screens and graphical user interfaces (GUIs) were just another project at Parc. At the time, developers probably never considered that people would one day use computers to create professional-looking typography and felt this one size fits all economical. Real quote marks are not straight, or neutered as some say, but face right or left to indicate whether they are opening or closing a quotation.

Typographer's quote marks   He said, "it's a 'guy's thing.'"

Inch marks   She said, "oh, that's so boring."

Figure 4-27: **Quotation and tick marks**

ADDITIONAL MARKS AND SYMBOLS

Most professionally created typefaces also include symbols for business, math, currency, and punctuation (e.g., accents and other diacritical marks used in many languages). For instance you might need the registered, trademark, or copyright symbols if you are producing DVDs of copyrighted material.

ENTERING SYMBOLS

Creating professional-looking typography takes a little work on a PC. The main problem is that the Windows keyboard is not set up easily to access the proper punctuation and other typographic symbols. You have two options when it comes to adding these characters.

- Copy and Paste the character from the Character Map utility.

- Memorize the character's Unicode equivalent, press the Num Lock key, press and hold the Alt key, and then enter the equivalent on the numeric keypad.

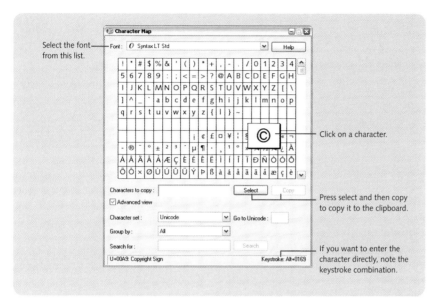

Select the font from this list.

Click on a character.

Press select and then copy to copy it to the clipboard.

If you want to enter the character directly, note the keystroke combination.

Figure 4-28: **Character Map Utility**

You can access the Character Map utility from the Start menu:
Start > All Programs > Accessories > System Tools > Character Map.

For your convenience, I have provided a Photoshop file with text layers containing these symbols. The text is set in Arial, but you are free to change the text properties in the file or copy the character(s) you need and change the properties later. Because this file follows the layer naming convention for menus, feel free to add the file to the Library palette (see [xref heading & page]).

The file, special-characters.psd, *is for copying and pasting text symbols. It is located in the* Design Goodies *folder on the book's DVD.*

Type Measurements

Besides having a classification system, a nomenclature, and a spectrum of styles, typography has a measurement system. This system mostly was based on the constraints of letterpress printing, or movable type. With this printing method, each letter of type is a single wood block or metal slug. These blocks are put together to form words, the words are spaced with letter space blocks to form lines, and strips of lead are placed between the lines to space multiple lines of text.

SIZE

The basic measurement of type is its size. With digital typography, type size is determined by the distance from the bottom of the descender to the top of the ascender.

Figure 4-29: **How type is measured**

 Although print design measurements are based on points and picas, Encore DVD measures type using pixels.

When determining text size, remember that the viewer of a DVD sees text differently than the reader of a book. The text on a printed page is probably a foot or two from the reader. The text on a DVD menu can be a foot or two from the reader if the DVD is viewed on a computer and the viewer is in front of it, but if the viewer is watching the DVD on a television or on a projected surface, the distance can be several to dozens of feet from the viewer. Given these conditions, it is important not to make your type too small because it will be illegible. Aesthetically speaking, text should not be too large because it can appear heavy handed. If you know the environment in which the DVD will be viewed, deciding on the appropriate text size is relatively easy because you can test how it looks with the medium the viewer will be using.

SPACING

All typefaces should have an em space and en space. The em space is a horizontal space that was originally determined by the width of an uppercase "M", but now it is equal to the font size. The em space is the widest continuous space available in a typeface. An en space is half the width of an em space. A normal character space is between a quarter and half of an em space. The em dash (—) and en dash (–) are determined by their corresponding spaces.

TRACKING

One point of confusion is the difference between tracking and kerning. Tracking is the addition or removal of uniform space between characters in a *range of text*. Loose or positive tracking spreads the words far apart; tight or negative tracking brings the words closer together.

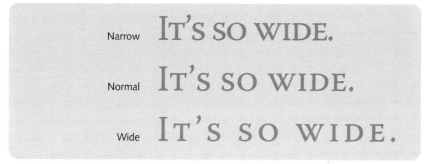

Narrow IT'S SO WIDE.

Normal IT'S SO WIDE.

Wide IT'S SO WIDE.

Figure 4-30: **Examples of tracking**

When to use Tracking

Many people ask, "When do I use tracking versus kerning?" I'd respond that there are no hard and fast rules, while advising that tracking is the power tool and kerning is a tool for making small adjustments.

You can apply only tracking or only kerning, or use both. Consistent optical space or even texture the objective. Text with an even texture is easier to read because the eyes move at a constant pace and are not interrupted by jarring spaces or cramped letter forms.

I use tracking in the following instances.

- *To fit body text*. In most cases, rewriting will solve this problem, but if text cannot be rewritten, apply tracking to see if this helps. Excessive tracking may cause overly-tight or loose spacing, making text hard to read.

- *To make adjustments when there isn't time to kern*. Often, tracking produces acceptable results. Remember, you can always undo it if it doesn't look good and make small kerning adjustments.

KERNING

Kerning is the space between *two* letter forms. Like tracking, loose or positive kerning adds space between two letters: tight or negative kerning, which bring the letter forms close together. Good kerning shows the same amount of optical space

In the days of lead type, a kern was the part of the letter form that extended beyond the type block.

between letter forms. Kerning letter forms so that the physical space is equal and legible (Figure 4-31).

Positive kerning **the day after next**

No kerning **the day after next**

Negative kerning **the day after next**

Figure 4-31: **Kerning examples**

When to use Kerning

- *When setting a headline or title in uppercase.* These text forms receive a lot of attention. Remember that uppercase has its roots in carved stone, and that each letter form is strong enough to stand alone. In this case, I normally do not trust tracking, so I kern the type for proper and consistent spacing.

- *When setting text for buttons.* Because viewers focus on the buttons of a DVD menu, it is important that the text look evenly spaced. More often than not, small type does not always render evenly at the coarse resolution of video.

- *When using a poorly spaced typeface.* Change the typeface if possible. But if a client has a corporate or required typeface, kerning and even tracking are the best way to deal with this problem.

LEADING

As mentioned earlier, varying widths of lead strips create the vertical space between lines of text in movable type. Because lead was used, this measurement is called leading. Leading is also referred to as interline spacing or line spacing, with leading and line spacing the two most popular. In digital typography, leading is measured as the vertical space between adjacent baselines. Leading and type size are related in fractional form when describing the two 9 point type on 12 point leading, or 9/12.

 The advantage of digital typography is that a whole number does not work like a decimal number might (e.g., 13.5 pixels of leading).

Good leading guides the reader's eyes effortlessly and without fatigue. Thus, the relationship between the type size and leading is crucial to making text legible. The problem occurs when lines of text have little to no leading. Although a headline or title can be interesting with little to negative leading, stifling a paragraph with negative or zero leading causes the eye to wander vertically and get "off track." Similarly, very loose leading makes it hard for the eye to transition from one line of text to another.

Typeface Technology and Formats

When moving designs across computers or exchanging files with colleagues or clients, you need to know what typefaces are used and their file format. These typefaces should be legally installed on all machines where menu design will take place.

Postscript, TrueType, and OpenType

Before Photoshop built Adobe's second tower in San Jose, Postscript built the first. Postscript is a page description language invented at Adobe that laser printers and offset presses use to produce printed material. The letter forms in a Postscript typeface are described mathematically by this language. If you have ever converted type to outlines in Illustrator, you can see how Postscript creates form with Postscript's Bezier curves, which is much different than with the brush or pen! Postscript type is the typeface format for professional designers and does not work cross platforms.

TrueType is a format developed by Apple and Microsoft and creates letter forms by quadratic, rather than Bezier, curves. Although some might argue the merits of one format over the other, I have relied on Postscript type because that is what I have always done. As long as the type is properly drawn and spaced, you should feel free to use whatever works for you.

Figure 4-32: TrueType, Postscript, and OpenType icons

OpenType was developed to solve some of this confusion. OpenType is essentially a wrapper technology that embeds Postscript or TrueType information into a single typeface. It also can contain thousands of characters in a single typeface, whereas the other two formats top out in the hundreds. With larger character sets, Asian languages can "fit" within a single typeface, and Roman typefaces can combine several type families into one. OpenType with the "Pro" designation have additional characters for more advanced typography. These additional characters can be accessed from the Character palette's flyout menu in Photoshop (Figure 4-23).

TYPEFACE FOUNDRIES

Garamond is not Garamond in all cases. Adobe Garamond, Stempel Garamond, and ITC Garamond are noticeably different interpretations of the French original. By knowing how to classify and examine type, you can tell the difference between Stempel Garamond, which is a good interpretation of the original, and ITC, which is a dated interpretation.

It is often said that type is like tea—you can never have too many varieties. New type, like new tea, can be refreshing. If you are looking for the latest varieties or a specific typeface, I've listed a few type foundries in Table 4-1 to browse.

Table 4-1: **Type Foundries**

FOUNDRY	TYPE OFFERING	FORMATS
Adobe Systems, Inc. http://www.adobe.com/type	Adobe licenses designs from other foundries but also has a collection of revival and new designs called Adobe Originals.	Postscript and OpenType
Berthold Type Foundry http://bertholdtypes.com	Berthold is an independent type foundry with an impressive collection of classical revivals.	Postscript and OpenType
Agfa Monotype http://www.monotype.com	Agfa purchased Linotype and Monotype, two of the larger type foundries. They have the largest collection of original type.	Postscript and TrueType
The Font Bureau http://www.fontbureau.com	The Font Bureau has a high-quality catalog of type from custom type development, as well as type developed for retail release.	Postscript and TrueType
Font Shop http://www.fontshop.com	The Font Shop has an eclectic mix of type and offers the Font Book, an up-to-date catalog of typeface designs from the past and the present.	Postscript and TrueType
The Foundry http://www.thefoundry.co.uk	A small type foundry that produces highly original typefaces that are more than just revival designs.	Postscript and TrueType
Emigre http://www.emigre.com	Perhaps the trendiest of the type foundries. They continue to create original type and revival designs with a unique spin.	Postscript, TrueType, and OpenType
Hoefler Type Foundry http://www.typography.com	Jonathan Hoefler and Tobias Frere-Jones have teamed together to produce type for private clients but also offer retail typefaces.	Postscript and TrueType
House Industries http://www.houseindustries.com	Another trendy foundry producing original typefaces and nostalgic revivals of period typographic styles.	Postscript and TrueType

Specifying Body and Display Faces

My favorite activity is choosing type for a project. This is a great time to visit the type foundries and see what is new, or to choose a typeface that is appropriate, but that I have not used before. In specifying type, consider the following questions, activities, and guidelines.

1. **Questions**
   - Is there a corporate typeface? If not, what typefaces seem stylistically suitable for the design? What conveys the mood and message? Do you hope your design will look old, new, rough, fresh, serene, fun?
   - Does the text need to be flexible? Will links have long names? Will there be a lot of onscreen text?
   - Does the typeface look legible at DVD resolution?
   - What are the hierarchical relationships between text elements? How can size, color, font family, and style create hierarchy?
   - Of the typefaces you have chosen, which have multiple styles?

2. **Activities:**
   - Pick a couple each of serif, sans serif and display typefaces.
   - Create studies in which you mix up to three styles from up to two typefaces.
   - When settled on a system, add size, color, and the imagery to the experiment. Create storyboard animations, do quick compositions in Photoshop.
   - Create three or four approaches. Print them out, look at them on screen, look at them on a television. Get the opinion of others around you.
   - Pick one approach and document it.

3. **Guidelines**
   - Keep your type experiments small and controlled. If each typeface is a single voice, it becomes clear that effective communication is created from fewer voices and not many.
   - Avoid mixing types that share the same classification and are similar. It fails to achieve variety and creates uneven texture because of the small differences in the type styles.
   - Do not fake type styles. Do not create fake bold, italic, small capitals, condensed, or extended type. It looks unprofessional and cheap and rarely does the job as well as type that is designed for the purpose.

- Apply the proper letter spacing and leading. Spacing that is overly tight or too loose creates poor texture and looks like mud on a television.

- Use proper punctuation. Careless punctuation is an obvious sign of amateur typography.

- Do not mix justification styles. Centered headlines and footers with flush left buttons is inconsistent.

- Be ready to break a rule, but do it for a good reason. Break more than two and you run the risk of committing bad typography to screen.

Type Included with Encore DVD

When I say Western, I mean the Roman alphabet.

After installing Encore DVD, you might notice that Adobe installs 58 Western typefaces. They include serif, sans serif, display, monospaced, and symbol typefaces.

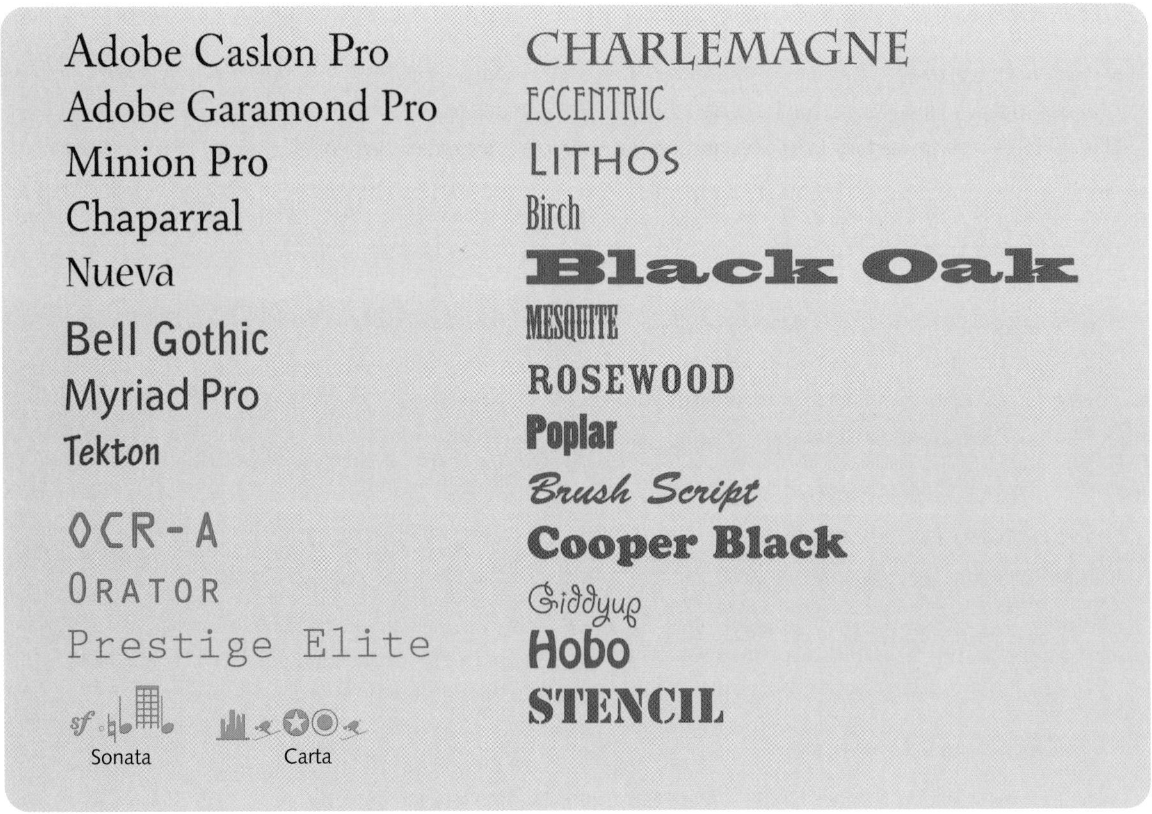

Adobe Caslon Pro
Adobe Garamond Pro
Minion Pro
Chaparral
Nueva
Bell Gothic
Myriad Pro
Tekton
OCR-A
ORATOR
Prestige Elite
Sonata   Carta

CHARLEMAGNE
ECCENTRIC
LITHOS
Birch
Black Oak
MESQUITE
ROSEWOOD
Poplar
Brush Script
Cooper Black
Giddyup
Hobo
STENCIL

Figure 4-33: **Type included with Encore DVD**

SERIF TYPE

The serif types installed include five typeface families totaling 22 styles: Adobe Caslon Pro, Adobe Garamond Pro, Minion Pro, Chaparral, and Nueva. These versions of Caslon and Garamond are revival versions created by Carol Twombly from historical designs.

SANS SERIF TYPE

The sans serif type installed comprises three typeface families totaling 14 styles: Bell Gothic, Myriad Pro, and Tekton. Bell Gothic is a Gothic or Grotesque sans serif. Myriad is an Adobe Original typeface with Humanist qualities reminiscent of Frutiger. Tekton was the greatest selling typeface of the early 1990s and was designed by David Siegel, who was one of the Web's first pundits on design. Although some people might raise their brows at classifying Tekton as a sans serif, one can argue that its roots in architectural lettering make it sans serif.

MONOSPACED TYPE

Monospaced type included in the installation are OCR-A, Orator, and Prestige Elite. OCR-A was created for bar codes and optical character recognition. When applied to a design, it connotes high tech or science fiction. Orator and Prestige Elite are two Slab Serif monospaced typefaces found on typewriters.

DISPLAY TYPE

Encore DVD includes a good variety of display type: Charlemagne, Eccentric, Lithos, Birch, Black Oak, Mesquite, Rosewood, Poplar, Brush Script, Cooper Black, Giddyup, Hobo, and Stencil. Use these faces for headlines or for buttons that are medium to large in size.

SYMBOL TYPE

Encore DVD also includes two symbol typefaces, Sonata and Carta, that are good for musicians and for people who require cartographic or international symbols.

 The musical notes in Sonata are good for subtitles that communicate music or singing.

The Purpose of Grids

Grids help establish order to a design. Order imparts emphasis and meaning to elements in the design. Grids, when applied across a series of menus, creates consistency, which in turn allows the viewer to remember button placement: consistency also facilitates production because text blocks, buttons, images, and video are standardized to fit the grid.

Screen Sizes

DVD menus, as mentioned in Chapter Two, have two sizes for both NTSC and PAL video standards. For convenience, I have listed them again in Table 4-2. The menu size and screen format is crucial in designing DVD menus because they dictate how much flexibility you have in creating a grid for the screen.

Table 4-2: **Screen sizes for NTSC and PAL video**

STANDARD	SCREEN FORMAT	PIXEL ASPECT RATIO[A]	RESOLUTION
NTSC	Standard (4:3)	Computer (1)	720 x 534
		DVD-Video (0.9)	720 x 480
	Widescreen (16:9)	Computer (1)	864 x 480
		DVD-Video (1.2)	720 x 480[b]
PAL	Standard (4:3)	Computer (1)	720 x 576
		DVD-Video (1.066)	720 x 576
	Widescreen (16:9)	Computer (1)	1024 x 576
		DVD-Video (1.42)	720 x 576

a.This column lists the pixel aspect ratio in parentheses.
b.Includes a flag that instructs the player to interpret the image as anamorphic.

Parts of a Grid

Grids in most computer programs are Cartesian grids; the grid is constructed by a single square unit. All columns and rows are the same size. A typographic or layout grid is different. It has the following parts: margins, columns, rows, and horizontal and vertical gutters. The margin is the space between the edge of the screen and the beginning of the grid. The margin should not be smaller than the video-safe margin. Columns are the vertical sections on the screen and have width. Rows are the horizontal sections on the screen and have height. Columns are equal in width and rows are equal in height. Gutters are the spaces between adjacent columns or rows and provide padding to help legibility. These too should be consistent in width and height. The space between two adjacent columns and two adjacent rows is a field.

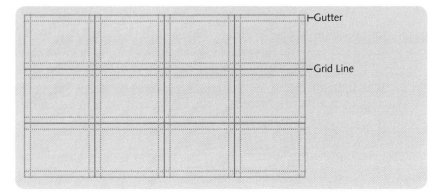

Figure 4-34: **Parts of a grid**

Items placed on the grid are not limited to one column. An object can occupy one, two, or three columns. Columns and rows that are consistent in width and height create uniformity, and the eye picks up on this internal order.

Video-Safe Margins

Title-safe and action-safe margins frame the video's visible safe zones. The title-safe margin is the inside square and is the guideline for placing text. You should not place important text outside of the inner square. The action-safe margin is a guide for important action, composition, and actors. No shots should be framed so that important elements in the shot are outside of the outer square.

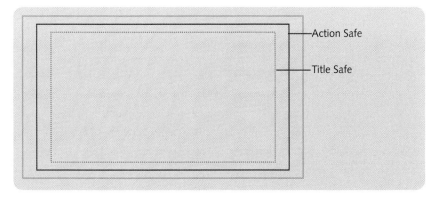

Figure 4-35: **Video-Safe Margins**

Photoshop 7 cannot show safe area margins, but Photoshop CS can optionally create guides in place of the margins.

Safe zones are required because the majority of consumer televisions have over scan, which crops the outer edges of the frame, allowing the center of the picture to be enlarged. To make things worse, the amount of overscan varies across televisions, which is why the safe margins are so important. At the very least, turn on the the safe area margins to ensure that your menus will display properly. For best results, preview your video on a television monitor connected to your computer.

 Encore DVD previews still menus on a television using a Firewire port. Certain Matrox RT cards offer more support for timeline and menu preview on a television.

Creating Grids

Before you create the grid, you need to understand the content. Ask the following questions before creating a grid.

- How many buttons will be on any given screen? Will the buttons be text only, image only, or have both text and image?

- Will there be associated imagery on the menu? Will the imagery be a collage or separate elements? Does the design require placement for a logo, company name, or project title?

- What are the text needs outside of buttons? Will it be a sentence or a short paragraph?

- What is the hierarchy of all the elements on the screen? Can they be divided into groups? What will be the most visually important item to present?

One approach to creating a grid is to place the most important design element by itself on the Photoshop file and determine how the grid supports it and additional content. Ask yourself what will be above and below it and what will be to the left and right of it? What are the spatial requirements for these elements? Create and space columns consistently. Create and space rows consistently. If everything does not fit harmoniously, resize the elements and the grid until they do. The height for gutters between rows should be the same as the leading. The width for gutters between columns should be large enough so the eye reads columns separately and easily. From this exercise, you also should have developed the size and placement of text, images, and buttons.

ESTABLISHING HIERARCHY WITH A GRID

Now that you have a grid, the process of creating hierarchy becomes easier. The grid system and the hierarchy is often created simultaneously. You rank the importance elements, group them by meaning if necessary, and then devise a grid to support these relationships. The elements that constitute the hierarchy are the title, any meaningful imagery or footage, primary buttons, secondary buttons if they are needed, and supplementary text and graphic elements.

All elements do not need to start in the same column. They can be staggered. Remember that grid uniformity ensures consistency and trains the eye. In applying the grid, it should not appear mechanical, but organic. This feeling is created by properly emphasizing each element by its placement, size, and color. The design should lead the eye through the design. Where is the opening or where does the eye begin and where does the eye end?

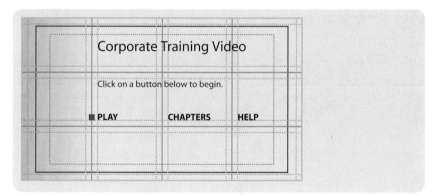

Figure 4-36: **Spanning columns in a grid**

Using Color

Color beautifies, but do not forget that it also creates mood and meaning. For instance, color can symbolize an idea, an event, or an entity. Think of red, white, and blue; red hot, green with envy. Do not let these or other cliches define color usage, but be aware that color has physical, political, psychological, and cultural connotations.

In communication and information design, the judicious use of color creates separation between elements, highlights important information, and communicates readiness. For instance, the sections in this book are color coded signal a change in subject matter.

Figure 4-37: **Color in information graphics**

The meaning of color can play a crucial part in user interface. Color is often used to indicate selection, activation, disablement, and whether or not something is a link. Color, however, should not be the only cue because some viewers with sight impairment cannot discern between colors. Color combined with a change in form, position, size, or other embellishment is a more effective way to communicate change.

Color Models

There are three common models for producing color: the color wheel, offset printing inks, and the color primaries of light.

SUBTRACTIVE COLOR MODELS

The color wheel and offset printing inks are both subtractive color models because combining their color primaries at full intensity theoretically creates black. In subtractive color models, adding color creates less color. A subtractive color model produces color by reflecting and absorbing color wavelengths. For instance, when you look at a color printout of yellow, the yellow is reflected and cyan and magenta are absorbed.

If you are only familiar with one of these models, it is most likely the color wheel. The color wheel is created by mixing three primary colors of red, yellow, and blue.

Mixing any two colors creates secondary colors, and the colors in between the secondary colors create tertiary colors.

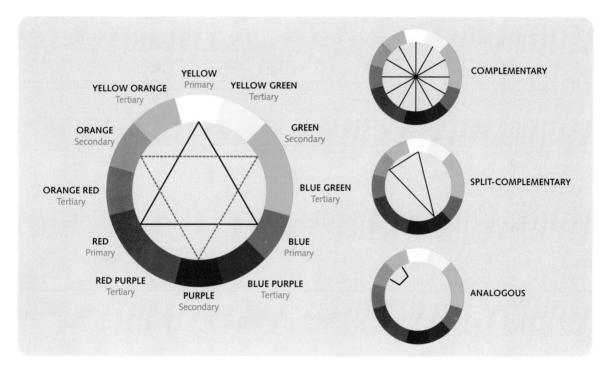

Figure 4-38: **Color wheel and color relationships**

RELATIONSHIPS ESTABLISHED BY THE COLOR WHEEL
The color wheel establishes fundamental color relationships. These are monochromatic, analogous, achromatic, complementary, neutral, and split complementary.

- *Monochromatic* colors share the same hue but vary in tint or shade. Tints are created by increasing a color's brightness or adding white, and shades are created by decreasing a color's brightness or adding black.

- *Analogous* colors are adjacent on the color wheel and are close in hue.

- *Achromatic* colors are shades of gray, black, and white.

- *Complementary* colors occupy opposite positions on the color wheel. Their hues are 180 degrees apart and can be thought of as two extremes. This effect helps create contrast that is rich and often symbolic.

- *Neutral* colors are formed from a single hue and varying amounts of the hue's complement.

- *Split complementary* colors are defined by the relationship between three colors: one color and the two that are adjacent to its complement. Just as its name implies, the first color splits the complement and takes the color on either side.

CMYK

Offset printing often uses CMYK (cyan, magenta, yellow, and black) to reproduce color. Each color is used for a specific plate of color. The plates are etched with halftone patterns, and when the plates combine on paper, they create tonal and color ranges.

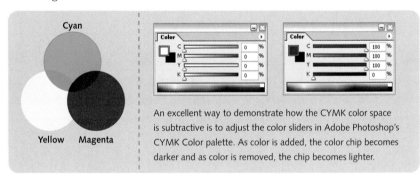

An excellent way to demonstrate how the CYMK color space is subtractive is to adjust the color sliders in Adobe Photoshop's CYMK Color palette. As color is added, the color chip becomes darker and as color is removed, the chip becomes lighter.

Figure 4-39: **Offset printing color model**

ADDITIVE COLOR MODELS

Television and computer monitors render color with red, green, and blue (RGB) light. This model is additive because when the three colors are equally combined to their full extent, they create white, which contains the full range of colors. This can be seen when white light is split with a prism or when rainbows are created by the refraction and reflection of light in water droplets.

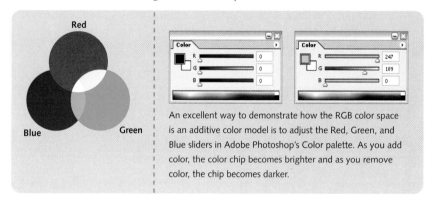

An excellent way to demonstrate how the RGB color space is an additive color model is to adjust the Red, Green, and Blue sliders in Adobe Photoshop's Color palette. As you add color, the color chip becomes brighter and as you remove color, the chip becomes darker.

Figure 4-40: **RGB color model**

In designing DVD menus, you will use RGB or HSB (hue, saturation, and brightness) color models. Rather than divide white by equal parts of red, green, and blue, HSB splits color by the color's hue, saturation, and brightness. Hue, or temperature as it's sometimes called, is the shade of color from warm to cool. Saturation is the color's intensity; crimson is high saturation, whereas dull gray colors have no saturation. Brightness, as it implies, is the color's lightness or darkness. The HSB color model is an effective model for creating tints and shades of a particular color.

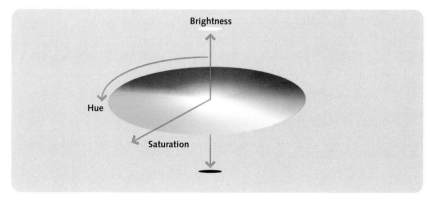

Figure 4-41: **HSB Color model**

COLOR RESOLUTION
Color resolution is not image resolution. Image resolution is the measure of how fine or detailed an image is. Color resolution is the number of colors available to

reproduce an image. The first personal computers had 1-bit black and white displays. In the late 1980s, grayscale displays became more prevalent. Grayscale monitors could reproduce 256 levels of gray when coupled with an 8-bit grayscale video card. As computer video technology improved and the first color displays were introduced, 8-bit or 256-color displays became prevalent.

Most computers today have displays that support 24-bit color, which reproduces approximately 16.7 million colors. Because each channel of color (red, green, and blue) is given 8 bits of color, 256 x 256 x 256 = 16,777,216 possible colors.

GAMUT

Gamut is the range of reproducible colors for a device. The gamut for a subtractive color model like offset printing is much smaller than that of an additive model like RGB, which is even smaller than that of the human eye.

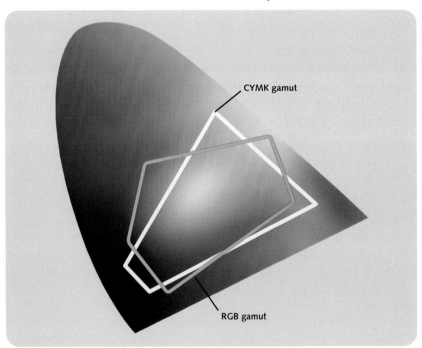

Figure 4-42: **Gamuts for additive and subtractive color models**

Color Sketches

When creating color sketches, consider the client's corporate identity guidelines. Think about the mood, the effect, and the message you are creating. What I find useful is creating color studies in Photoshop. I create a file with a solid white background, and I mix colors with the Color palette and put fill colors that I like onto squares, each on its own layer. I move the colors next to each other, create new ones, turn old ones off, and compare the new colors, then create a gray background and see how the colors compare to the background.

After determining how many colors are needed, I create a set of tints and shades for each color. Tints are created by adding brightness and shades by removing brightness. Document these colors by entering the RGB model for each color. Specify how each color is used. Is it the text color, background color, or highlight color?

Imagery

The subject of imagery could fill an entire book, or perhaps a dozen books, so I will cover the subject only briefly. Ask yourself the following questions when thinking about imagery.

- *Medium and technique*. How are the images created? Are they photographs or illustrations? Are they computer generated, like 3-D animation? Are they enhanced with filters, color processing, masking, or collage? Whatever the technique, be consistent.

- *Symbolism and iconography*. Do the images have any significance or meaning beyond being backgrounds? Certain techniques, such as masking and color processing, can enhance an image's symbolic power.

- *Composition*. Composition should be pleasing and should direct the eye to important information. Where does the eye begin, and where do you want the eye to end or focus?

- *Combining type and image*. How will the text and imagery work together? Will they overlap or have their own spaces on the screen? Will the imagery be in the background or occupy a space defined by the design grid?

Animation

Animation approximates motion through sequential imagery. Good animation, however, has spirit, cleverly exaggerates reality, and enhances a menu's aesthetic, communication, and entertainment value.

This chapter presents the following topics

- The animation process
- Animation principles
- Common properties to animate

Where possible, I have related the topics discussed to designing motion menus for DVDs.

The Animation Process

The animation process begins with an idea that is turned into a script or a storyboard. After the concepts presented in the storyboard are approved, animation and production begins. Test renders and animatics turn into fully rendered animations that are then imported into Encore DVD and integrated with other assets to create menus.

Coming Up with an Idea

Ideas for animating motion menus differ from project to project and have to be appropriate to the material being shown. For example, it would not make sense to show something depressing with material that is meant to be inspirational. Often, the client will have some ideas, but do familiarize yourself with the content before beginning to animate because it might provide you with a host of ideas.

The process of animating a motion menu is a superset of the design process. Before anything is animated, something needs to be designed, photographed, shot on video, recorded on audio tape, or illustrated. But before any of this happens, the animation has to be scripted. I like to start by jotting down a few ideas:

A postcard of Alamo Square rotates onto screen. When it is in place, the menu title slides down from above. The buttons fade into place.

With these few ideas, I might draw a quick sketch or a couple of thumbnail sketches that begin to form a storyboard (Figure 5-1).

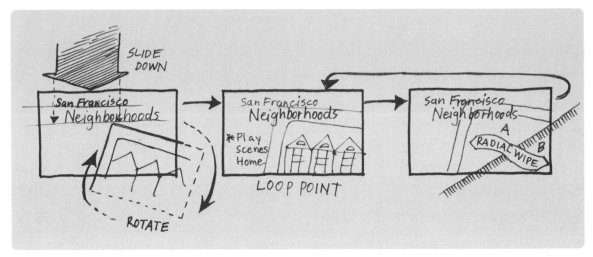

Figure 5-1: **Ideas and thumbnail sketches**

If you need other forms of inspiration, I would suggest looking at the title sequences that start most films. Over the last 15 years, there has been a real renaissance in film title design that has influenced most of the motion graphics seen on television, DVD menu design, and the Internet.

Creating Storyboards

Whereas words communicate verbally, a storyboard communicates a narrative visually. Storyboards are another development of early animated films. Directors of live-action films took notice and quickly adopted the storyboard format by hiring artists to create storyboards from their scripts. Storyboards present an idea conceptually. They indicate the camera angle, the position of characters and objects, the lighting to be used, and the action that occurs. This versatility makes them the most useful planning tool for animation.

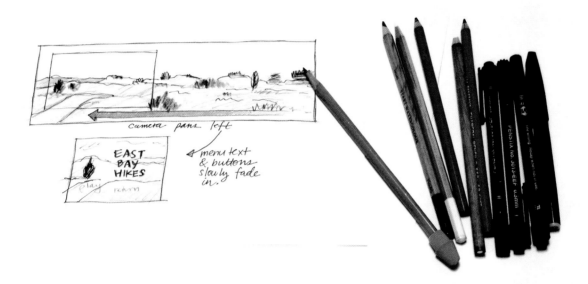

Figure 5-2: **Storyboards**

Although DVD menus are short in length, storyboards can still help in the planning and production process because they are easy and quick to produce. Keep a supply of pencils and felt tip markers of varying thicknesses. I usually begin by sketching lightly in graphite and then adding tone with charcoal. A can of spray fixative is suggested if you do not want the charcoal to smudge. Additional detail or thinner dark accents can be applied with felt markers or india ink and brush.

You can also use a drawing program such as Illustrator to create storyboards quickly. Figure 5-3 shows a system that you can use to specify movement, transition, and other visual properties in your storyboards.

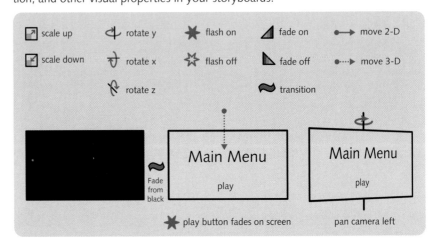

Figure 5-3: **Storyboard notation**

 These symbols and storyboard templates are available in the Animation folder. They are in Illustrator and PDF format.

Animation Principles and Menu Design

The *Principles of Animation* were developed by Frank Thomas and Ollie Johnston (1981, NYC, Hyperion) at Walt Disney in the early 1930s, and they remain a valuable set of criteria for developing and critiquing any animated work.

Figure 5-4 is an abridged version of their list that I have tailored to the design of DVD motion menus. I have taken the liberty to organize the 12 principles into three categories: variation, combination, and execution. Variation creates the difference between one frame and the next. Combination makes animations more complex by animating more than one property simultaneously. Execution is how the animation is presented and how it is received by the viewer. It is important to remember that all of these principles work together in creating effective animation.

VARIATION	COMBINATION	EXECUTION
Timing	Secondary Animation	Line of Action
Exaggeration	Anticipation	Staging
Squash and Stretch	Overlap	Craft
Ease In and Out	Follow Through	Appeal

Figure 5-4: **Principles of animation**

Timing

Timing, or pacing, is the speed at which the animation moves. Quick pacing implies sudden actions and behavior, whereas slow pacing implies slower movement. When a heavy weight falls off of a table, quick pacing shows the severe gravitational pull on the weight. When a feather falls of the table, slower pacing shows the floating properties of the feather.

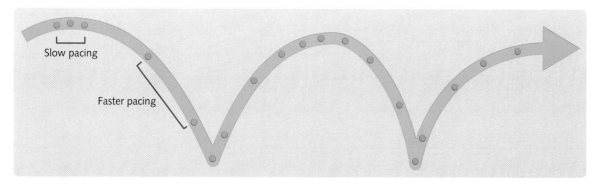

Figure 5-5: **Timing of a bouncing object**

KEYFRAMES AND INBETWEENS

A keyframe is an instance of any animated object at a specific time. Any animation requires at least two keyframes. The use of keyframes was developed when film studios and animation houses began creating animated films with teams of animators. Lead animators would draw the "key" poses for a character, and assistant animators would complete the sequence by drawing the frames in between. With digitally created motion graphics, you set the values for keyframes, and the computer creates the frames in between. In Figure 5-6, the red points on the path are keyframes and represent key positions in the ball's movement.

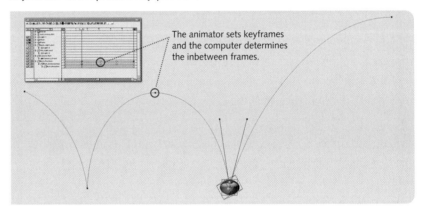

The animator sets keyframes and the computer determines the inbetween frames.

Figure 5-6: **Keyframes**

Exaggeration

As mentioned earlier, animation is an approximation of motion and emotions. When this approximation is pushed well beyond the bounds of reality, it becomes exaggeration, and it begins to be a parody of reality. Not only can exaggeration be funny, but it also adds emphasis. Figure 5-7 examines the difference between adding exaggeration to a bouncing ball and not applying any exaggeration.

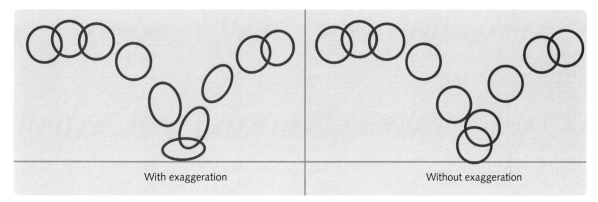

Figure 5-7: **With and without exaggeration**

Squash and Stretch

Squash and stretch is an animation technique that illustrates the effects of gravity and force on volume and shape. To see this principle in real life, observe the flexing of muscles, or watch a rubber ball bounce. Notice how the arm swells when the bicep is contracted and how a ball flattens and widens as it hits the ground.

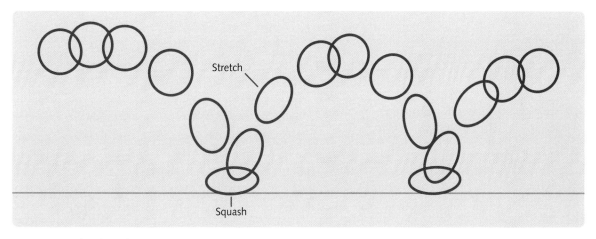

Figure 5-8: **Squash and stretch**

Squash and stretch adds believability and interest to animation. In order for squash and stretch to be truly believable, the volume of an object is consistent even though the shape changes.

I cannot tell you which principles are appropriate to apply to your menu design, but I have listed examples of how they can be applied to headline text, buttons, or any design element in a menu. Common techniques are a rolling baseline, objects that inflate or deflate, and bouncing objects.

Ease In and Ease Out

In reality, objects in motion do not accelerate or decelerate suddenly because they resist gravity, wind, liquid, or other physical barriers. For instance, a car does not reach 25 miles per hour immediately upon ignition, nor does it stop suddenly when the brakes are pressed. A car, like most moving objects, gradually accelerates and decelerates. Ease in and ease out mimic the gradual transition between movement and stillness.

In addition, the mass of the object determines how quickly it gets into motion and stops; heavier objects take more time, and lighter objects take less time. Think about a Ping-Pong ball. Once you hit it, it zips across the table, but if you catch it in your hand, the ball immediately ceases to move. Now imagine that the ball is made of lead. It would take a great deal of force to get it up to speed. Once you caught it, your hand would recoil because the momentum of the ball is transferred to your hand.

If you are using almost any professional animation or motion graphics tool, ease in and ease out are always on by default. At times you might find you need to make small adjustments to how an object animates. If your animation package offers an editable graph view of the animation data, called a velocity graph, you can use this view to sharpen (speed up) or flatten (slow down) an ease in or ease out sequence.

Secondary Animation

Secondary animation is, as its name implies, secondary to the primary movement. For example, as a woman turns her head, the main movement is her head turning, but there is more going on: her hair moves, her eyes may blink, and her facial expression might change. You might not use secondary animation in your motion menus unless your design involves character animation, in which case you are probably very aware of these principles.

Anticipation

Anticipation in traditional character animation is the visual cue the animator creates to show you something is about to happen. It is a transition from one story point to another. It can be shown physically, emotionally, or both. For example, a cartoon rocket ship launches. In this example, the rocket does not go from stationary to liftoff, but ignition and exhaust are shown before it bolts off into the wild blue yonder, escaping gravity.

| Stationary | In anticipation of the launch, the rocket swells as the engines ingnite. | The rocket stretches as it achieves lift off. |

Figure 5-9: **Anticipation**

Anticipation can best be used when setting transitions between a menu's introductory animation and its loop point or between the end of one menu and the beginning of another.

Overlap and Follow Through

Two principles, overlap and follow through, determine how animation unfolds. For instance, when a stadium crowd performs the "wave," they do not all rise and fall at the same time—the movement between members of the crowd is delayed. This delay is the overlap. Follow through is the full range of motion that each member of the crowd completes. They do not simply stand and sit, but they bend over, raise their torso, and then raise their arms in one fluid movement.

If a piece of animation appears too jarring or abrupt, consider how overlap and follow through could be added. For example, if text slides on screen from the left, perhaps the last few letters can drag a little before catching up with the first ones.

Line of Action

The line of action is the path the animation takes in a scene. For motion menus, this can easily be defined in a storyboard sketch. When there are multiple lines of action, consider contrasting the lines to add dynamism.

MOTION PATHS

A motion path is the continuous line of movement that an object follows over time. If an object has more complicated movement, the path will not be straight, as in the case of the bouncing (Figure 5-10).

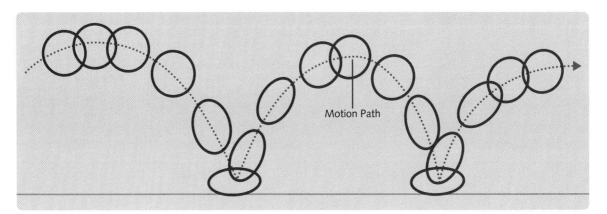

Motion Path

Figure 5-10: **Motion path for a bouncing ball**

 When storyboarding animation, include the motion paths on the storyboards. This will help facilitate the planning process.

Staging

Staging is the composition of the animated elements. Good staging shows animation at its best, and poor staging will weaken the animation's presentation no matter how good the animation is. Think of staging as showing the animated element's "good side." Figure 5-11 shows two examples of staging. The first frame is poorly staged—the menu's title is rotated too much, is not very legible, is too low on the screen, and appears cramped. The second frame shows the title in perspective, but it is still legible and makes better use of the space.

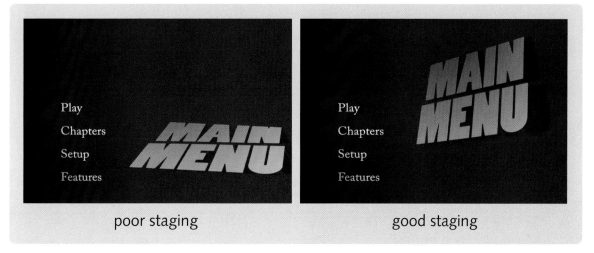

Figure 5-11: **Staging**

Solid Drawing or Craft

In traditional two-dimensional cell animation, solid drawing skills are stressed because well-executed drawing looks better. This is not to say the drawing has to be realistic, but it should have clearly established contrast between straight and curved lines, and the shapes drawn should be indicative of motion, gravity, and mass.

You will probably not have to draw your animation by hand, and you will likely use software to animate your motion menus. In this case, solid drawing translates to craft or production value. Good craft results from understanding design principles and having the skills to apply them in a way that is thoughtful and deliberate. For example, a skilled carpenter produces work that is seamless, smooth, and robust, whereas a weekend warrior produces work that shows its gaps, is rough, and is wobbly.

Appeal

Appeal, like delight, is an intangible quality that is measured by the viewer's satisfaction and enjoyment. Animation has appeal when the viewer finds humor or surprise. Some viewers can appreciate the complexity of motion and effects and enjoy the precision and craft of the design. Appeal is a measurement of the viewer's overall experience.

Animation Properties

In order to create animation, an object has to change in some manner. For example, it has to move, grow or shrink, change color, blow up, disappear, or melt. When any of these things occur, the object's characteristics change. These characteristics are geometric properties such as position, scale, rotation and visual properties such as opacity, color, and form.

ANCHOR POINT

In most animation programs such as After Effects, the anchor point is by default in the center of the object.

When animating an object, its animation is determined by its anchor point. Like an anchor thrown in the water, an anchor point influences how an object moves. When the anchor point for an object is offset from the center, the object maintains a relative distance from the anchor point.

The anchor point is also the origin for scale and rotation. When scaling an object, it grows from the anchor point. When rotating an object, the object rotates around the anchor point.

Figure 5-12: **The x in the middle of the floral element is the anchor point**

DIMENSION

Two-dimensional animation occurs in the x (left to right) and y (top to bottom) planes. If you remember the early video game Pong, this is perhaps one of the simplest forms of two-dimensional animation. An animated object is animated in two or three dimensions.

Today, creating perspective-accurate animation has been simplified with three-dimensional animation and compositing programs such as After Effects. This is achieved by simulating the characteristics of three-dimensional forms and camera properties such as depth of field and focus. Three-dimensional animation occurs in the x, y, and z planes.

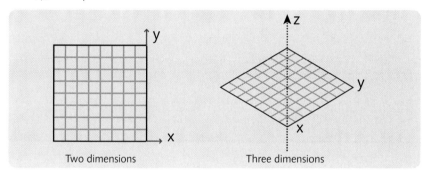

Two dimensions　　　　　Three dimensions

Figure 5-13: **Dimension**

POSITION AND DIRECTION

These are the most fundamental aspects of animation. In the simple scene of a ball bouncing, the ball's position changes from one frame to another. Its direction is a result of the animator approximating or exaggerating mass and gravity. Over time, the direction can be described as a motion path. With dimension, this path can occupy two or three dimensions.

SCALE

Animating the scale of an object over time typically indicates that the object is growing or shrinking or coming closer to or going farther away from the camera. When animating words or graphic elements, however, animating the scale of something can signify importance and hierarchical relationships. Objects can be scaled proportionally or in any combination and amount of the *x*, *y*, and *z* planes.

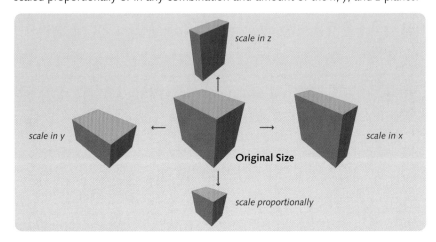

Figure 5-14: **Animating scale**

ROTATION
When an anchor point is at the center of an object and the object is rotated, the object spins in place. However, if the anchor point is located to the right of the object, the object will swing like a pendulum.

OPACITY
Opacity is an object's transparency. If an object is 100 percent opaque, it is solid; if it is 0 percent opaque, it is invisible. Opacity is commonly animated when creating transitions. For example, one image is layered on top of another image and revealed as it goes from transparent to opaque.

COLOR AND TEXTURE
The color and texture of an object can be animated to indicate selection, importance, hierarchy, or physical characteristics such as temperature, speed, or mood.

FORM
Animating an object's form or shape can suggest motion, speech, or a transformation in meaning. For example, the ball that bounces is flatter when it hits the ground, speech phonemes are created by animating the shape of the mouth, or an arrow can change from pointing up to pointing down to signify a change in direction.

Null Objects

A null object has all the transformation properties of a visible object but does not render. The use of null objects is a production technique that saves time, ensures consistency, and adds flexibility. The process begins by linking other objects to a null object. The linked objects then inherit properties from the null object so that as you animate the null object, the linked objects animate in the same fashion.

For example, if you want several stars on a screen to rotate at the same speed, it is faster to animate a null object and link the stars to it than to animate the stars independently. If the animation has to be changed, the null object is changed and all the stars follow suit. In addition, several null objects can be combined and linked together to create a framework for positioning complex objects or cameras. Figure 5-15 shows a top that has two null objects that assist in animating the top's position and rotation.

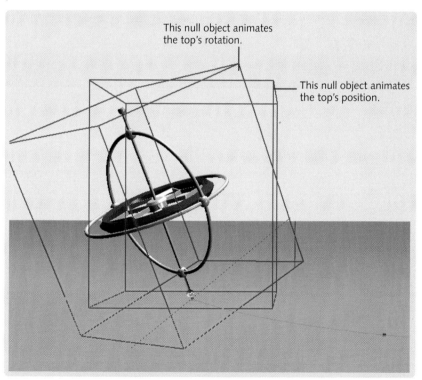

Figure 5-15: **The top has two null objects: one for position and the other for rotation**

Animating the Camera

Many animation programs can now position and move a camera in three-dimensional space. In many cases, camera moves that would have been costly and require expensive camera support equipment is now achievable within an NLE or compositing application. With this facility, however, is the risk of moving the camera poorly. Whiplash zooms and pans are indicative of poor camera movement and often do more to distract and confuse than to entertain and inform.

In some cases, only the camera needs to be animated. For example, a common effect in documentaries is panning and zooming slowly into important elements of a scene. In other situations, moving the camera subtly while animating an object can create interesting effects (Figure 5-16).

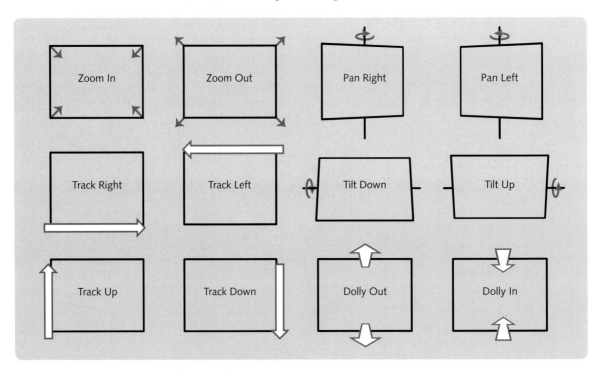

Figure 5-16: **Camera movements**

Pans and tilts are created when rotating the camera horizontally or vertically on a center of rotation. When the camera is rotated on a long arm that moves up and down, this is a crane movement. Zooms are created when the lens is adjusted to increase or decrease the magnification for a shot. Zooms should not be confused with a dolly move. To dolly the camera is to physically move the camera in the *z* plane or into or out of a shot. Tracking is moving the camera left or right or up or down. Sometimes panning is mistaken for tracking, but pans and tilts are rotating the camera, whereas tracking involves moving the camera in the *x* or *y* plane without rotation.

Transitions

Transitions are often used at edit points in a video or film sequence. Likewise in a motion menu, transitions can be used around the loop point or can be used to introduce or exit from a menu. These segments that occur before or after the menu are referred to as "intro and exit loops" or "interstitials." Whatever you call them, in most cases, these segments will employ some form of transition if they do not join together seamlessly. Common transitions are dissolves, effects, and no transition or "jump cuts" (Figure 5-17).

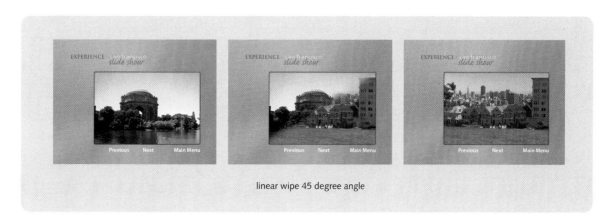

linear wipe 45 degree angle

Figure 5-17: **A linear wipe transition at a 45 degree angle from right to left**

 Adobe Premiere Pro and After Effects have many transitions that can be applied. Look in the Effects tab in either product and experiment on clips to see how they look.

The Encore DVD User Interface

This chapter is a complement, not a replacement, for the Adobe Encore DVD User Guide. It covers only the interface as it applies to menu design and it provides additional explanation on certain aspects of the user interface.

Project, Menus, Timelines, and Disc Tabs

The New Project Settings dialog then appears and you are prompted to choose NTSC or PAL as the television standard. After choosing a standard, the Encore DVD main window appears. This window contains the Project, Menus, Timelines, and Disc tabs.

To create a project, choose File > New Project or press Ctrl+N.

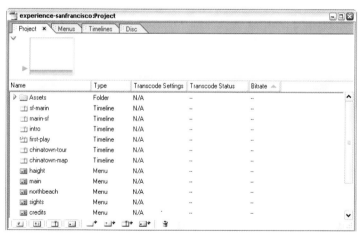

Figure 6-1: **Encore DVD's main window**

 Closing the main window does not always close the project. The project closes when all windows (Menu Editor, Timelines, etc.) are closed or when Shift+Ctrl+W is pressed.

Project Tab

To open or close the Project tab, choose Window > Project or press F9.

Assembling a DVD begins by creating menus and timelines from imported assets: Photoshop menus, audio, video, and still images. If you have used the Project window in Adobe After Effects or Adobe Premiere Pro, Encore DVD's Project tab will appear familiar because it is essentially the same window found in the other two products. It is used to organize assets, menus, and timelines and is the first tab shown.

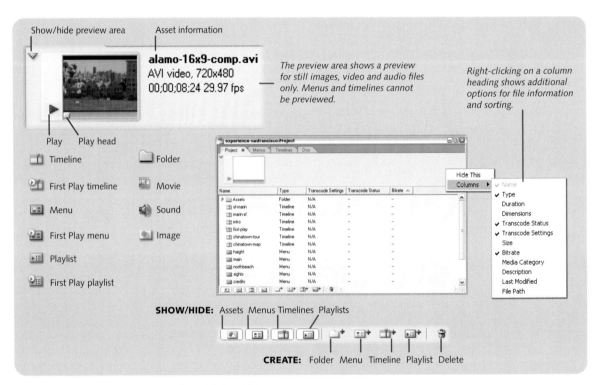

Figure 6-2: **Project tab**

IMPORTING ASSETS

The video, sound, and image files destined for the final DVD need to be imported into Encore DVD. Encore provides several convenient methods for importing assets:

- Choose File > Import or press Ctrl+I
- Double-click on empty space within the file list

- Drag and drop from Windows Explorer

- Right-click on empty space within the file list and choose Import…

The file types that are supported in Encore are listed in Table 6-1.

Table 6-1: **Supported file formats for assets**

ASSET	SUPPORTED FORMATS	NOTE
Video	• Elementary MPEG-2 streams • Program streams with MPEG-2 • VOB files • Microsoft AVI • QuickTime	Any file that can be played back in DirectShow, except those with an extension of .QT or .MOV.
Audio	• MPEG audio, layers I and II • WAV with PCM audio inside • AIF	Any file that can be played back in DirectShow, except for those with an extension of .qt or .mov
Menu	• PSD	Layered Photoshop files should follow Encore DVD's layer naming convention for best results.
Image	• Photoshop (.PSD) • Windows bitmap (.BMP) • JPEG (.JPG) • Targa (.TGA) • Portable network graphic (.PNG) • Tagged image file format (.TIF) • Graphic interchange format (.GIF) • MPEG (.MPG or .M2V)	

 Encore DVD 1.5 offers limited support for QuickTime files. If source material is in QuickTime, Encore DVD transcodes it automatically.

Elementary MPEG-2 streams and VOB files are various flavors of MPEG-2 that MPEG-2 encoders create when translating from other digital video formats. Elementary streams are files that contain only video or only audio. You import these files into Encore and add them to the video and audio tracks of a timeline, or pick them separately for a menu background. VOB (Video Object) files are MPEG-2 files that have been mastered to a disc.

IMPORTING AND CREATING MENUS

Layered Photoshop files need to follow Encore DVD layer naming conventions for best results.

Menus that are created in Photoshop need to be imported as a menu, not as an asset, because assets are always imported as *flat* images. The layer sets structure within the Photoshop file needs to be preserved for linking buttons. The two ways to import Photoshop files as a menu are to

- choose File > Import as Menu... or
- right-click on empty space within the file list and choose Import as Menu....

When you import a menu, you are actually copying the Photoshop file to the project's menu directory and creating a reference to the copy in the project file. This is different from creating a reference to the original Photoshop file. Encore DVD creates a copy because it embeds important metadata regarding the menu in the file, so when you make changes to the menu in Photoshop, you are not editing the original file you imported, but the copy that Encore DVD created.

For more information on the Library palette, see page 156.

Creating a menu within Encore DVD is just as easy as importing a menu. Menus that are created in Encore DVD are based on the default menu template in the Library palette. To create a menu,

- click the New Menu icon, 🖿⁺, at the bottom of the Project window
- choose Menu > New Menu
- right-click on empty space within the file list and choose New Menu
- press Ctrl+M.

CREATING TIMELINES

To create timelines in Encore DVD,

- click the New Timeline icon, 🖿⁺, at the bottom of the Project window
- choose Timeline > New Timeline
- right-click on empty space within the file list and choose New Timeline
- press Ctrl+T.

CREATING PLAYLISTS

To create playlists in Encore DVD,

- click the New Playlist icon, 🖿⁺, at the bottom of the Project window
- choosing File > New Playlist
- right-click on empty space within the file list and choose New Playlist.

FILES AND IMPORTANT DATA LINKED IN A PROJECT

The Project tab shows menus, timelines and imported assets, but it does not show other information that is particular to a project and can be imported or exported from the project. Figure 6-3 explains the relationships between all elements in a project.

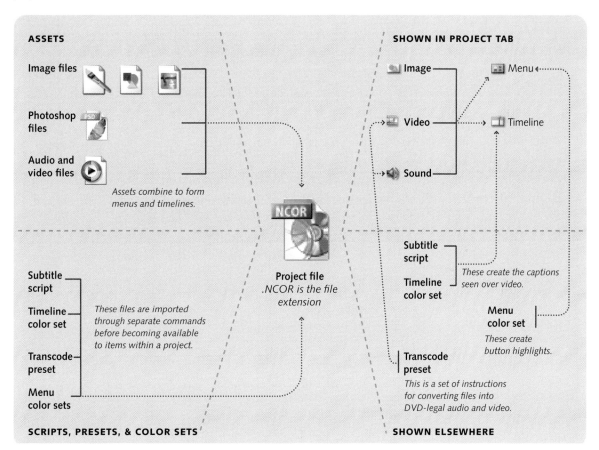

Figure 6-3: **Project structure**

Assets are the items brought into the project to create menus and timelines. Scripts, presets, and color sets are XML or binary files that define such things as text subtitles for video timelines, settings for transcoding video and audio, and color palettes for button highlights and subtitle text colors.

This book does not cover transcoding or subtitles. Refer to the Encore DVD User Guide.

 Subtitle text cannot be exported, but transcode presets and menu and timeline color sets can be.

SORTING AND FILTERING THE VIEW

The Project, Menus, and Timelines tabs have similar sorting functions (Figure 6-4).

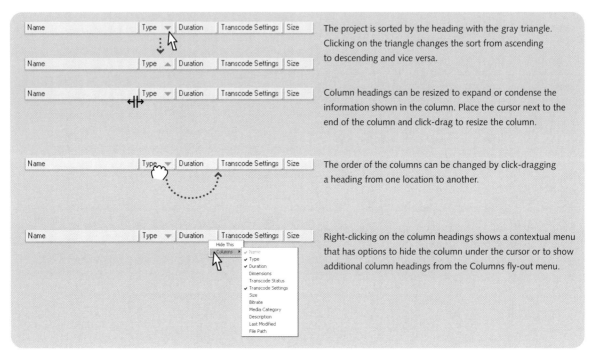

The project is sorted by the heading with the gray triangle. Clicking on the triangle changes the sort from ascending to descending and vice versa.

Column headings can be resized to expand or condense the information shown in the column. Place the cursor next to the end of the column and click-drag to resize the column.

The order of the columns can be changed by click-dragging a heading from one location to another.

Right-clicking on the column headings shows a contextual menu that has options to hide the column under the cursor or to show additional column headings from the Columns fly-out menu.

Figure 6-4: **Column sorting**

Project Column Headings

Name: Item name.

Type: Item filetype.

Duration: Duration in hh:mm:ss:ff or hh;mm;ss;ff. "Still Image" is shown for images.

Dimensions: Item dimensions. It is listed as Width x Height. "--" is shown for audio.

Transcode Status: The asset transcode status. Options are "Needs Transcoding," "Transcode Pending," "Transcoding Now," "Transcoded," and "Don't Transcode."

Transcode Settings: The asset transcode preset. "Auto" is shown if no preset is chosen.

Size: Asset size in KB (kilobytes), MB (megabytes), or GB (gigabytes).

Bitrate: The transcoded or estimated playback datarate for assets.

Media Category: The item's category. Options are: Image, Video, Audio, or Video & Audio.

Description: Informative text for the item entered in the Properties palette.

Last Modified: Asset modification date.

File Path: The asset location on the hard disk. Shown in italics when the asset is offline.

Filtering the Project tab's view hides or shows particular types of assets. Clicking the first three buttons at the lower left of the Project window toggle the display of assets, timelines, and menus (Figure 6-5).

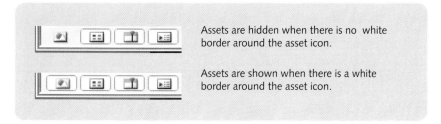

Assets are hidden when there is no white border around the asset icon.

Assets are shown when there is a white border around the asset icon.

Figure 6-5: **Filtering buttons**

CREATING FOLDERS AND ORGANIZING ASSETS

The Encore DVD Project window facilitates organizing large projects with folders. These folders are not folders on the hard drive, only in the project. For example, you can create a folder named "slide show images" for all the photos used in slide shows and then create folders within it for different slide shows—"city," "bridge," "neighborhoods," and "golden gate park." You can use folders to keep track of your progress. For example, menus without links are placed in the "unfinished" folder whereas menus are placed in the "finished" folder. Folders are opened or closed by clicking on the triangle, to the left of the folder icon.

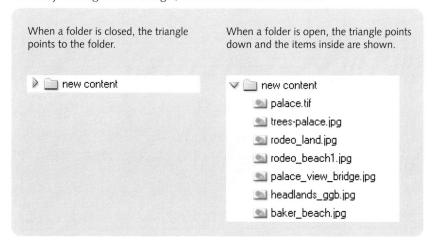

When a folder is closed, the triangle points to the folder.

When a folder is open, the triangle points down and the items inside are shown.

Figure 6-6: **Open and closed folders**

To rename an asset, folder, menu, or timeline choose Edit > Rename or press Ctrl+R. Renaming an asset will not change its name on the hard disk.

SETTING THE FIRST PLAY ITEM

See First Play on page 25 for more information.

The first play is the first item shown when the final disc begins to play. By default, the first play is the first menu, playlist, or timeline created. It is easily changed to something else by selecting the menu, playlist, or timeline you want to be the first play and doing either: choosing File > Set as First Play or right-clicking on the selected item and choosing Set as First Play.

PROJECT TAB CONTEXTUAL MENUS

Encore DVD has three contextual menus in the Project tab. One is shown when you right-click on an item, another is shown when right-clicking on a folder, and the third appears when you right-click on empty space, the space at the bottom of the window or between rows or columns. (Figure 6-7)

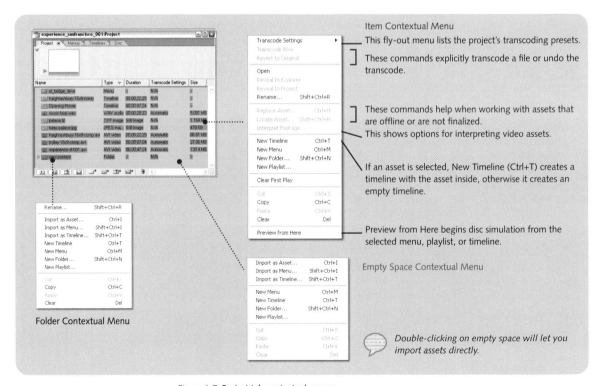

Figure 6-7: **Project tab contextual menus**

Menus and Timelines Tabs

The Menus and Timelines tabs facilitate DVD authoring by providing a global view of authoring properties related to menus and timelines.

To show the Menus tab, choose Window > Menus or press F1.

MENUS PANE

The Menus tab contains two panes: the top pane lists all the menus and the lower pane lists the buttons in the selected menu. (Figure 6-8)

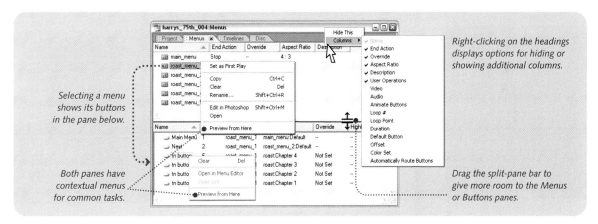

Selecting a menu shows its buttons in the pane below.

Both panes have contextual menus for common tasks.

Right-clicking on the headings displays options for hiding or showing additional columns.

Drag the split-pane bar to give more room to the Menus or Buttons panes.

Figure 6-8: **Menus tab**

Menus Pane Column Headings

Name: Menu name.

End Action: The destination shown when the menu finishes.

Override: Replaces the End Action property of the menu's destination.

Aspect Ratio: The menu's relative proportion of width to height.

Description: Informative text for the menu.

Video: A video shown in the background.

Audio: An audio file played for the menu.

Animate Buttons: Animated buttons are created from chapter points. The duration is set to the menu's duration.

Loop #: The number of times a menu plays before stopping or showing the end action.

Loop Point: The position in time from where the menu loops.

Duration: Menu duration.

Default Button: This is the number of the button selected when the menu is shown.

Offset: Specifies a whole number that is added to the sequential number of each button in the menu.

Color Set: The color set used for the menu.

Automatically Route Buttons: Automatically calculates the routing between buttons.

BUTTONS PANE

The Buttons pane (Figure 6-9) shows all the selected buttons in the selected menus from the Menus pane. You likely will use this pane the most when authoring large projects.

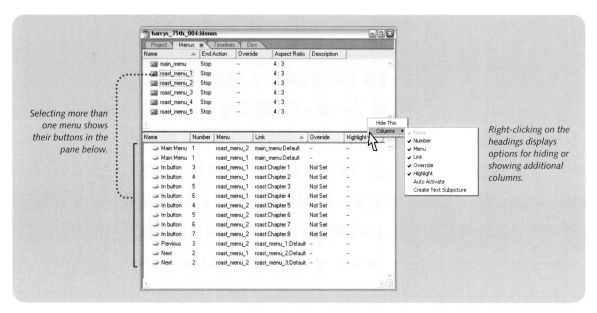

Selecting more than one menu shows their buttons in the pane below.

Right-clicking on the headings displays options for hiding or showing additional columns.

Figure 6-9: **Buttons pane**

Buttons Pane Column Headings

Name: Button name.

Number: Button number. Important when selecting a button with a remote control's number keys.

Menu: The menu that contains the button. Useful when selecting buttons across menus.

Link: The destination shown when the button is pressed.

Override: Replaces the End Action property of the button's destination.

Highlight: The color group used for the button selected and activated colors.

Auto Activate: When set, the button's Link property is shown immediately when the button is selected.

Create Text Subpicture: When set, this automatically creates a text subpicture with text layers for a button.

TIMELINES PANE

The Timelines tab, like the Menus tab, consists of two panes. The top pane lists all timelines in a project. When you select one or more timelines in the top pane, the lower pane lists only the chapters in the selected timelines.

To show the Timelines tab, choose Window > Timelines or press F11.

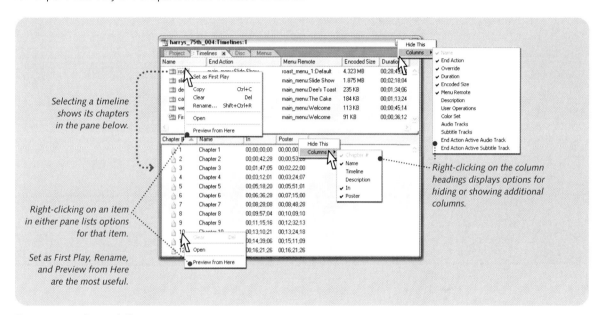

Selecting a timeline shows its chapters in the pane below.

Right-clicking on an item in either pane lists options for that item.

Set as First Play, Rename, and Preview from Here are the most useful.

Right-clicking on the column headings displays options for hiding or showing additional columns.

Figure 6-10: **Timelines and Chapters panes**

Timelines Pane Column Headings

Name: Timeline name.

End Action: The destination shown when the timeline finishes.

Override: Replaces the End Action property of the timeline's destination.

Duration: Timeline duration.

Menu Remote: This link is shown when the Menu key on a remote control is pressed while this timeline is playing.

Encoded Size: The size of the timeline after transcoding, or how large it is estimated to be after transcoding.

Description: Informative text for the timeline entered in the Properties palette.

User Operations: User operations are the actions accessible with a DVD remote control. Options are "All Permitted," "None Permitted," or "Custom."

Color Set: The color set used for the timeline.

Audio Tracks: The number of audio tracks in the timeline.

Subtitle Tracks: The number of subtitle tracks in the timeline.

End Action Active Audio Track: The audio track targeted in the End Action property.

End Action Active Subtitle Track: The subtitle track targeted in the End Action property.

.

CHAPTER POINTS PANE

Although the Chapter Points pane acts in a similar fashion to the Buttons pane, it is not used as often. If your video segments follow a rigid format, you might want to set chapter point properties globally. Figure 6-10 on page 133 shows the column headings and contextual menu for the Chapter Points pane.

Chapter Points Pane Column Headings

Name: Chapter point name.

Chapter #: Chapter point number.

Timeline: The timeline containing the chapter.

Description: Informative text for the chapter entered in the Properties palette.

In: The position in time where the chapter point.

Poster: The position in time of the frame representing the chapter point. By default, this is the same as the In point.

Sorting and Filtering the View

The spreadsheet-like appearance of the Menus and Timelines tabs provides a powerful way to modify attributes with the Properties palette. You can even change attributes of several selected items in a single operation, which might not seem useful now, but if you ever have to open a dozen menus to change a common Link property, you will appreciate this capability.

USING THE PROPERTIES PALETTES

When you select an item in the Menus or Buttons panes, the item's properties appear in the Properties palette. This is important because the Project, Menus, and Timelines tabs are *read-only* views that cannot be edited directly. You need to select an item in one of these tabs and then edit links, names, or whatever in the Properties palette.

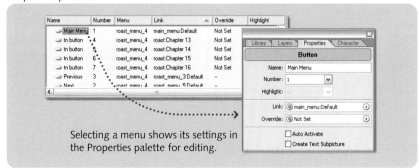

Selecting a menu shows its settings in the Properties palette for editing.

Figure 6-11: **Using the Menus tab with the Properties palette**

CHANGING THE PROPERTIES OF SEVERAL ITEMS AT ONCE

Say you design two Main Menus for a client. You like the first design and have authored the project to link to this menu. The client decides at the last minute that he likes the second design. This is a common problem. Rather than open up every menu and change the main menu link tediously, use the Menus and Buttons panes to change all the Main Menu links quickly. (Figure 6-12)

To show the Properties palette, choose Window > Properties or press F5

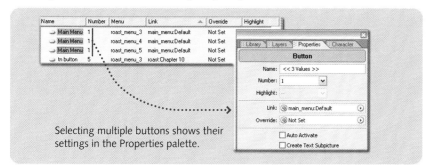

Selecting multiple buttons shows their settings in the Properties palette.

Figure 6-12: **Changing several link properties at once**

Now this is not just limited to button links. It can be used for any property you would need to change globally. The following examples illustrate how this feature can save you time.

* Set the color sets used across all the menus in the project.

* Set the highlight group across buttons that exist in different menus.

* Set the button number consistently across menus for buttons that are similar.

* Set the Create Text Subpicture property for buttons that have text.

* Set the Menu Remote property to the same link for timelines that originate from the same menu.

* Set the color sets used for subtitle text across all timelines in the project.

Disc Tab

The Disc tab contains a graph showing space occupied by DVD-Video and DVD-ROM content for the current project, as well as functions for adding DVD-ROM

To show the Disc tab, choose Window > Disc or press F12.

content, setting copy protection and region codes, checking links, and burning a disc. (Figure 6-13)

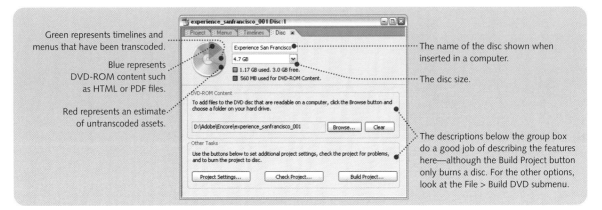

Green represents timelines and menus that have been transcoded.

Blue represents DVD-ROM content such as HTML or PDF files.

Red represents an estimate of untranscoded assets.

The name of the disc shown when inserted in a computer.

The disc size.

The descriptions below the group box do a good job of describing the features here—although the Build Project button only burns a disc. For the other options, look at the File > Build DVD submenu.

Figure 6-13: **Disc tab**

SETTING THE DISC SIZE

The size of the target medium is under the disc name text field. The disc size is used to calculate transcoding parameters and to track whether a project is too large for the target media. The options are:

- **650 MB**: CD-R media. CD-R media is playable on most computers, but not on all set-top boxes.

- **700 MB**: CD-R media. Same as above.

- **3.95 GB**: DVD-R for authoring media.

- **4.7 GB**: (DVD-5) DVD-writable media such as +R, -R, +RW, and -RW.

- **8.54 GB**: (DVD-9) A dual-layer DVD-Video disc. Dual-layer discs require access to a Digital Linear Tape (DLT) tape drive. You then send the DLT to a replication facility.

- **Custom…**: Reveals a text field for entering a new capacity in gigabytes. Use this to create a volume on a hard disk for kiosk playback.

READING THE DISC GRAPH

The disc graph represents the space used on the disc. It works in conjunction with the disc size drop-down box. Color coding shows the following.

- Space used by encoded assets in the DVD-Video zone (Green)

- Space used by unencoded assets in the DVD-Video zone (Red)

- Extra ROM files (Blue)

- Free space (Clear)

ACCESSING ADDITIONAL PROJECT SETTINGS

Set the least frequently accessed disc properties, such as region codes and copy protection settings, with the Project Settings dialog.

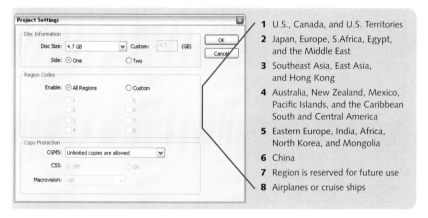

1 U.S., Canada, and U.S. Territories

2 Japan, Europe, S.Africa, Egypt, and the Middle East

3 Southeast Asia, East Asia, and Hong Kong

4 Australia, New Zealand, Mexico, Pacific Islands, and the Caribbean South and Central America

5 Eastern Europe, India, Africa, North Korea, and Mongolia

6 China

7 Region is reserved for future use

8 Airplanes or cruise ships

Figure 6-14: **Project Settings dialog**

Project Settings

Disc Size: See page 136.

Side: This side of the disc the project is on. This is enabled only for sizes meant for replication, that is, 4.7 and 8.5 GB discs.

Region Codes: All Regions allows playback anywhere. When Custom is chosen, any combination of the regions can be set.

CGMS: Also known as Copy Generation Management System or Copy Guard Management System. This prohibits copies or limits the number of sequential copies. Options are: No copies are allowed. (CSS and Macrovision are enabled), One copy is allowed (CSS and Macrovision are

disabled), Unlimited copies are allowed (CSS and Macrovision are disabled).

CSS: Options are: "CSS Off" or "CSS On." CSS encrypts video data by embedding decryption keys that are only readable from the original disc. When copies are made, the decryption keys are not added and the video is scrambled during playback.

Macrovision: Options are Macrovision Type I, II, III, or Macrovision Off (the default). Macrovision prevents recording DVDs to an external source such as a VCR by disrupting the recording signal between the two devices. If you plan to use Macrovision ask the replicator about the royalties involved.

Region codes, CGMS, CSS, and Macrovision are only for projects intended for replication and are not possible on DVD±R media.

ADDING DVD-ROM CONTENT

To add DVD-ROM content to a project, choose a folder containing content intended for the final disc and choose File > Specify DVD-ROM Folder..., or click Browse... in the Disc tab. Anything can go on the DVD-ROM portion of the disc, such as HTML, PDF, or other computer-readable or -executable files. The workflow is as follows.

1. Create a folder for the DVD-ROM content.

2. Place content inside this folder. This can be done at a later time, but do it prior to building the project.

3. Choose File > Specify DVD-ROM Folder... or click Browse... in the Disc tab.

    – A standard Windows Browse for Folder dialog appears. Navigate to and choose the folder with the DVD-ROM content and click OK.

    – The folder is chosen and is listed in the Disc tab as the DVD-ROM content folder.

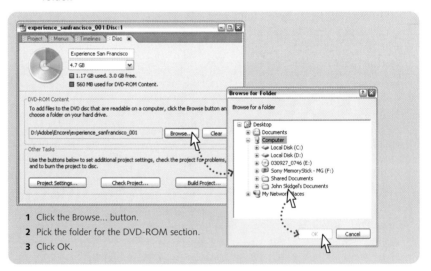

Figure 6-15: **Selecting a folder for DVD-ROM content**

CHECKING LINKS

The Check Links dialog lets you search for authoring mistakes such as

- invalid links (button, end action, and override)

- orphaned timelines and menus.

To show or hide the Check Links dialog, choose Edit > Check Links... or press Shift+Ctrl+L.

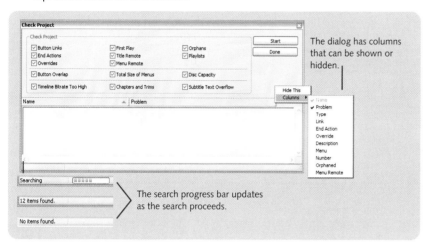

Figure 6-16: **Check Project dialog**

The Check Project dialog can also locate buttons, end actions, and override end actions that don't have a link specified. This dialog is also displayed before building a project, and it is a good idea to run a few searches to make sure the disc has all the links you need. The workflow is as follows.

1. Choose File > Check Project..., click the Check Project... button in the Disc tab, or press Shift+Ctrl+L.

    - The Check Project dialog appears.

    - Select the appropriate Search for options and click the Start button.

    - The status bar shows the word "Searching" and a progress bar.

2. If errors are found:

    - The status bar lists the number of errors found.

    - When an item has more than one error, click its disclosure triangle, ▶, to list the errors.

    - Select an entry (or entries) and fix them in the Properties palette.

Double-click an item in the list to open it. For example, double-click a button to show it in the Menu Editor window.

3. If no errors are found, the search pane remains empty and the status bar reads "No items found."

4. When finished, click Done to close the window.

The Menu Editor

The Menu Editor is for designing menus, previewing subpicture highlights, and linking and routing buttons. Encore DVD uses the Photoshop file format for menus. This means all your layers are imported and you are free to move layers and edit text. The Menu Editor window works in conjunction with the Properties palette for setting links and with the Layers, Library and Tool palettes.

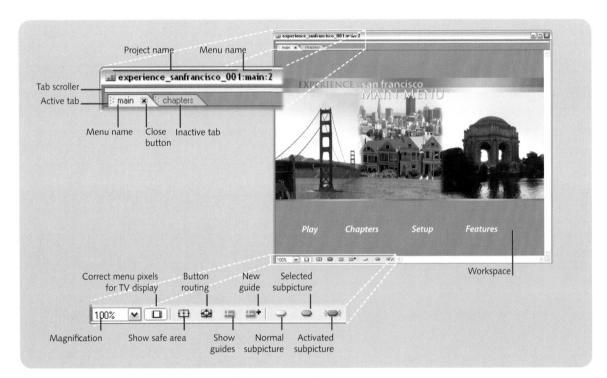

Figure 6-17: **The Menu Editor window**

Managing Multiple Menus

The Encore DVD Menu Editor can contain one or more menus simultaneously. Like the After Effects Composition window, it uses tabs to organize multiple menus within the window. The active tab appears brighter than the inactive tabs and is drawn on top. The active tab is closed by clicking the Close button, ☒. Tabs can be dragged outside of the current Menu Editor window to create a new window and can be dragged into another window to conserve space. If you have many menus open in one window, the tab scroll bar becomes available. (Figure 6-17)

Menu Editor Viewing Options

At the bottom of the Menu Editor window are several options for viewing a menu. There are controls for enlarging the display, showing safe area guides, routing buttons, and previewing button highlight states. Figure 6-17 on page 140 shows this area. Descriptions of the controls follow.

ZOOM LEVEL

This drop down box sets the magnification level for the current menu. The zoom level presets range from 25 to 400 percent. Custom zoom levels can be set up to 1600 percent by typing the value and pressing Enter.

CORRECT MENU PIXELS FOR TV DISPLAY

This toggle lets you preview how the menu will appear on a television (the default) or it shows the menu's actual dimensions. Adobe Encore DVD proportionally scales menus that do not conform to the project's television standard.

SHOW GUIDES

This displays guides that were created in Photoshop or in Encore DVD.

NEW GUIDE

This displays the New Guide dialog box. Guides created in Encore DVD are viewable in Photoshop.

Guides

Guides help align and position text, buttons, and shapes. In Encore DVD 1.5, there is added support for showing, hiding, snapping to, and locking guides created in Photoshop. Guides can also be edited and created in the Menu Editor window. Guides are specific to the menu in which they are created. They are not shared across menus in a project.

- To create a guide, click the New Guide button, ▦⁺, or choose View > New Guide... After the guide is created, you can move the guide by placing the cursor over the guide and click-dragging it to a new location.

- To remove a guide, drag it beyond the edge of the Menu Editor window. To remove all guides from a menu, choose View > Clear Guides.

- To show or hide guides, click the Show Guides button, ▦ , or choose View > Show Guides.

- To snap objects to guides, choose View > Snap To Guides. To turn off snapping, choose this menu option again.

SHOW SAFE AREA

The Safe Area button toggles the title- and action-safe area margins, which is the reliably visible area when viewed on a television. You should keep text elements within the inner guide and important motion within the outer guide. Click the Show Safe Area button, ⊞ , or choose View > Show Safe Area.

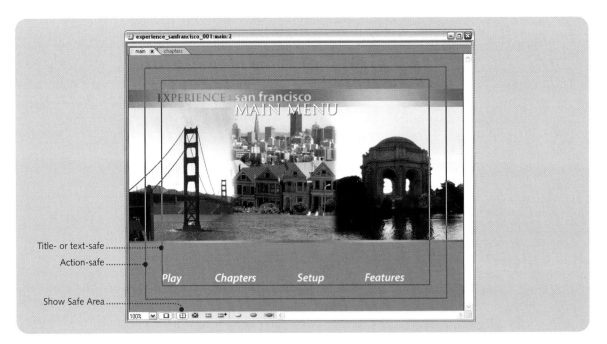

Figure 6-18: **Safe area guides**

BUTTON ROUTING

This button displays the routing between buttons in a menu. Click the Display Routing button, 🖼 , or choose View > Show Button Routing.

See Button Routing on page 17.

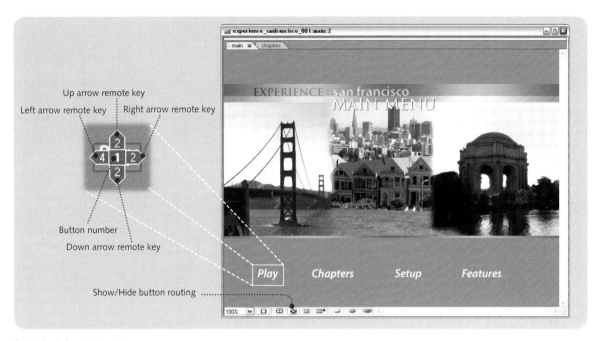

Figure 6-19: **Button routing**

SHOWING BUTTON HIGHLIGHT STATES

The last three buttons on the right bottom of the Menu Editor window (Figure 6-17) are for showing button highlight states. Clicking on any of these buttons will show the state for all the buttons onscreen.

See Subpictures on page 12 if you need a refresher course on how subpictures create button highlights.

The Show Normal State button, 😑 ,displays the subpicture graphic for the normal state. The Show Selected State, 😑 , displays the subpicture graphic for the selected state. The Show Activated State, 😑, displays the subpicture graphic for the activated state.

To hide the subpicture states, choose View > Show Menu Image or press Ctrl+2.

 Button routing and the state buttons are mutually exclusive and cannot be shown simultaneously.

Menu Color Set Dialog

For more information on color sets, see page 14.

The Menu Color Set dialog is used to manage the highlight colors shown for a menu's selected and activated button states. Encore DVD creates a color set called an automatic color set for each menu. You can, however, create and apply color sets, import color sets from previous projects, and export color sets for future projects. A project can have multiple color sets but a menu can use only one of these sets.

Automatic Color Sets

Encore DVD creates a color set automatically when a menu is imported from Photoshop by deriving and simplifying the colors found in each button's subpicture layers. Encore DVD creates an automatic color set for menus only (not timelines) at key times: when imported, when buttons are added or removed from the menu, when buttons are renumbered, and during the build process. This set is shown in the menu's Properties palette.

Note the following attributes of automatic color sets.

- A menu's automatic color set is not a global color set available to other menus, but is maintained internally within a menu. An automatic color set cannot be shared with other menus.

- An automatic color set is shown in the Menu Color Set dialog, but it is not editable. It can, however, be copied and the copy can be edited. The Color Set dialog displays an automatic color set only when a menu with an automatic color set is the current menu.

- Automatic color sets are created by examining the button layer set closest to the background layer and then examining the remaining buttons above it.

- See page 171 for more information.

- The normal color group is always set to be fully transparent. The Selected state colors for highlight group 1 are derived from the colors and opacity in the first button's (=1), (=2), and (=3) layers. The colors for the Activated state are set to be the same as the Selected state. Opacity for each color is also set for automatic color sets. The opacity comes from the layer opacity of the (=1), (=2), and (=3) layers. The opacity values created are converted to the closest of 16 opacity values supported by the DVD specification.

- The colors of the following buttons are compared and set to highlight group 1 if they match; otherwise they are used to create highlight group 2 in a similar fashion. The remaining buttons are compared to both highlight groups and set to the one they match. If they do not match either, they are set to highlight group 1.

- The Highlight Group property is disabled for buttons inside a menu with an automatic color set.

- When the menu is assigned to a global color set, the automatic color set is removed from the menu, but it is recreated when Automatic is chosen in the menu's Properties palette.

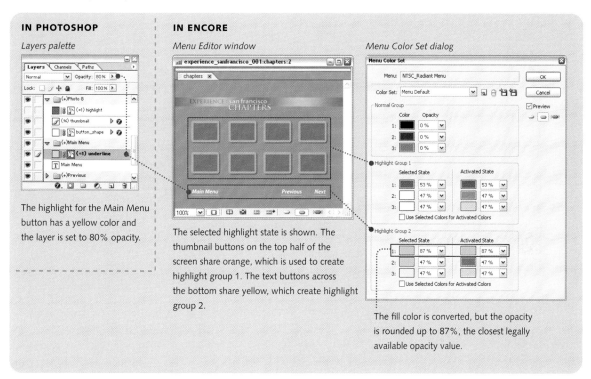

IN PHOTOSHOP

Layers palette

The highlight for the Main Menu button has a yellow color and the layer is set to 80% opacity.

IN ENCORE

Menu Editor window

The selected highlight state is shown. The thumbnail buttons on the top half of the screen share orange, which is used to create highlight group 1. The text buttons across the bottom share yellow, which create highlight group 2.

Menu Color Set dialog

The fill color is converted, but the opacity is rounded up to 87%, the closest legally available opacity value.

Figure 6-20: **Automatic color set workflow**

MANUALLY CREATED COLOR SETS

You create color sets with the Menu Color Set dialog. The dialog has three groups: one group for creating the normal or unselected button state and two distinct highlight groups that both have Selected and Activated color states (Figure 6-21).

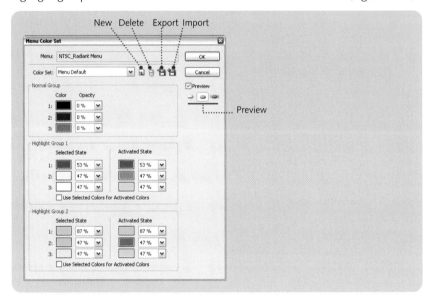

Figure 6-21: **Menu Color Set dialog**

Menu Color Set Controls

Color Set: The named project color sets.

Normal Group box: Colors used in the Normal state for all buttons.

Color swatch: Button state color.

Opacity: Button state opacity.

Highlight Group 1 box: The first of two color options.

Use Selected Colors for Activated Colors checkbox: Sets the Activated State Colors to the same as the Selected State Colors.

Highlight Group 2 box: The second of two color options.

OK: Saves any changes made and closes the dialog.

Cancel: Does not save changes and closes the dialog.

Preview: Previews the button states in the current menu.

New button: Displays a dialog for naming the color set.

Export button: Displays a dialog box for exporting the color set.

Import button: Displays a dialog for loading a color set.

Tool Palette

Although Encore DVD's Tool palette has fewer tools than Photoshop's, it has the tools used for viewing, selecting, and editing objects in the Menu Editor's workspace. Figure 6-22 shows the Tool palette and lists accelerator keys for selecting tools.

To hide or show the Tool palette, choose Window > Tools or press the Tab key. Pressing Shift and Tab keys will hide all palettes but keep the Tool palette onscreen.

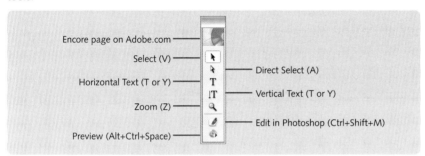

Encore page on Adobe.com
Select (V)
Horizontal Text (T or Y)
Zoom (Z)
Preview (Alt+Ctrl+Space)
Direct Select (A)
Vertical Text (T or Y)
Edit in Photoshop (Ctrl+Shift+M)

Figure 6-22: **Encore DVD Tool palette**

How to use the tools.

- Use the Select tool, ➤ , to move or scale buttons and layer sets.

- Use the Direct Select tool, ➤ , to move or scale a layer within a button or layer set.

- Use the text tools, T and ⏐T, to create horizontal and vertical text.

- Use the Zoom tool, ⚲ , to adjust the magnification level.

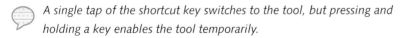 *A single tap of the shortcut key switches to the tool, but pressing and holding a key enables the tool temporarily.*

The Edit in Photoshop and Preview buttons are not tools; they are commands. Edit in Photoshop will transfer the current menu to Photoshop for editing. Preview launches the Project Preview window.

Selecting and Moving Objects

When you select a layer set in Encore DVD, a blue border is drawn around it. On each of the corners and midpoints of this border are handles for resizing the layer set. Click-dragging a layer set from within the border will move the layer set to a new position.

SELECTING OBJECTS

When you select a layer within a layer set, you see two borders: one for the selected layer and another for the layer set. The layer has resize handles, but the layer set does not. The layer set's border is helpful because it helps you see that that the layer is part of a layer set, (some layers can exist at the top level and not be in a layer set) and you can see how the button's highlight region will change if you move the layer beyond the layer set's current bounds.

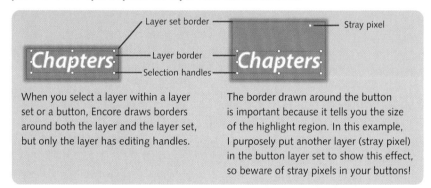

When you select a layer within a layer set or a button, Encore draws borders around both the layer and the layer set, but only the layer has editing handles.

The border drawn around the button is important because it tells you the size of the highlight region. In this example, I purposely put another layer (stray pixel) in the button layer set to show this effect, so beware of stray pixels in your buttons!

Figure 6-23: **A layer within a button or layer set**

 Selecting items in Encore DVD is different than in Photoshop. In Photoshop, you link items before moving or scaling them. In Encore DVD, you select the first item and then press Shift or Control and select the next item.

MOVING AND SCALING OBJECTS

With Encore DVD, you can make last-minute changes to designs created in Photoshop or design menus from scratch. To move an object, select it and click-drag it from within its selection handles to a new location. To scale an object, select it and click-drag one of its six selection handles to resize it. To flip an object, select the object and Choose > Object > Flip Horizontal or Object > Flip Vertical.

In addition, you can right-click on the object and choose one of the flip commands from the contextual menu.

 Encore DVD does not support rotating or freely distorting layers. To do this, choose Edit > Edit in Photoshop or press Shift+Ctrl+M.

Properties Palette

Many of the objects (menus, buttons, timelines, clips, chapters, etc.) within a project have attributes. When an object is selected, the Properties palette displays its attributes. Most of the attributes are editable, which makes this palette an indispensable tool in DVD authoring. Different properties are available, depending on the current selection. There are properties for: the disc, menus, buttons, playlists, timelines, chapters, video, audio, still, and subtitle clips, and assets.

To view the Properties palette, choose Window > Properties or press F5.

 I am only going to cover Menu, Button, Timeline, Playlists, Chapter, and Disc properties. For the other Properties palettes, see the Encore DVD User Guide.

Using the Link Control

Several attributes in the project are links of two types: DVD authoring or asset links. To facilitate setting links, Encore DVD has a control that is similar to GoLive's link control or After Effects' pickwhip control.

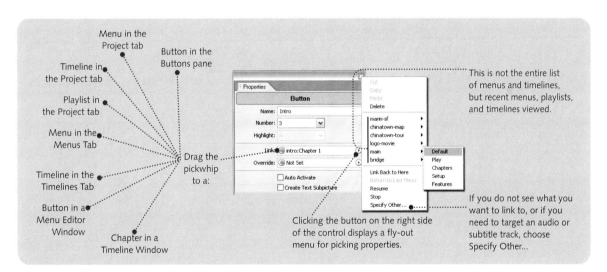

Figure 6-24: **Using the link control**

 The link controls used to set a menu's video and audio background only have pickwhip controls.

To view a menu's properties while in the Menu Editor, choose Edit > Deselect All or press Shift+Ctrl+A.

Menu Properties

The Menu Properties palette is displayed when a menu is selected in the Project or Menus tab. It is also displayed when there is no selection in the Menu Editor. When working in the Menu Editor, you use the Properties palette to set DVD-related properties for the menu and buttons. To see the properties for a button, select it with the Select tool.

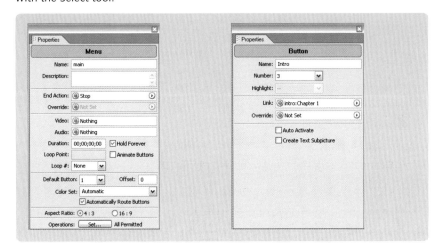

Figure 6-25: **Menu and Button Properties palettes**

Figure 6-26: **Menu properties**

PROPERTY	EDITABLE	DESCRIPTION
Name	Yes	The menu name.
Description	Yes	Informative text for the menu.
End Action	Yes	The destination shown when the menu finishes. Possible attributes are in the form of menu:button, timeline:chapter point, playlist, or Stop.
Override	Yes/No	Replaces the End Action property of the menu's destination. Possible attributes are in the form of menu:button, timeline:chapter point, or Not Set. This is not editable when the button's link has not been set.
Video	Yes	The video played in the menu's background. Possible attributes are Not Set or a video asset.
Audio	Yes	The audio played for the menu. Possible attributes are: Not Set, or an audio file in the project.
Duration	Yes	The menu duration. Attribute is in minutes;seconds;frames.
Hold Forever	Yes	Holds the menu forever. When the menu is set to Hold Forever, the attributes set in End Action, Override, and Duration are ignored.
Loop Point	Yes	The position in time from where the menu loops. Attribute is in minutes:seconds:frames. Drop and non-drop frames are supported.

PROPERTY	EDITABLE	DESCRIPTION
Animate Buttons	Yes	When set, animated buttons are created from the chapter point. The duration is set to the menu's duration.
Loop #	Yes	The number of times a menu plays before stopping or going to an end action.
Default Button	Yes	The number of the button selected when the menu is shown.
Offset	Yes	Specifies a whole number (0 or greater) that is added to the sequential number of each button in the menu.
Color Set	Yes	The color set used for the menu.
Automatically Route Buttons	Yes	When set, Encore DVD automatically calculates the routing between buttons. See page 17 for more information.
Aspect Ratio	Yes	Specifies whether the menu has a 4:3 or 16:9 aspect ratio.
User Operations	Yes	The permitted operations a user can do while the menu is present.

Button Properties

The Button Properties palette shows the attributes of the selected button.

Table 6-2: **Button Properties palette attributes**

PROPERTY	EDITABLE	DESCRIPTION
Name	Yes	The button name.
Number	Yes	The button number. Selecting a new number switches the numbers between the current button and the button that had the number previously. This is used when selecting a button with the remote control number keys.
Highlight	Yes/No	The color group used for the button. Used for selected and activated colors. This is not editable when the button's menu has an automatic color set.
Link	Yes	The destination shown when the button is pressed. Possible attributes are in the form of menu:button, timeline:chapter point, or Not Set.
Override	Yes/No	Replaces the End Action property of the button's link. Possible attributes are in the form of menu:button, timeline:chapter point, playlist, or Not Set. This is not editable when the button's link has not been set.
Auto Activate	Yes	When set, this causes the button's Link property to be shown immediately after selecting the button.
Create Text Subpicture	Yes	When set, this automatically creates a text subpicture for a button with text layers. The subpicture is created at the same position as the (=1) layer.

TImeline Properties

The Timeline Properties palette shows the attributes of the current timeline.

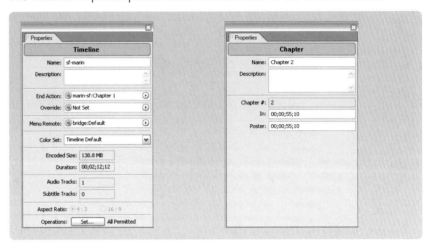

Figure 6-27: **TImeline and Chapter Properties palettes**

Table 6-3: **Timeline Properties palette attributes**

PROPERTY	EDITABLE	DESCRIPTION
Name	Yes	The timeline name.
Description	Yes	Informative text for the timeline.
End Action	Yes	The destination shown when the timeline finishes. Possible attributes are in the form of menu:button, timeline:chapter point, playlist, or Not Set.
Override	Yes/No	Replaces the end action property of the timeline's end action. Possible attributes are in the form of menu and button, timeline and chapter point, playlist, or Not Set. This is not editable when the button's link has not been set.
Menu Remote	Yes	The link shown when the Menu key is pressed on a remote control while this timeline is playing.
Color Set	Yes/No	The color group used for the subtitle text.
Encoded Size	No	The size of the timeline after transcoding or its estimated to be after transcoding. To adjust the size of the timeline, modify the transcoding preset for the audio and video clips.
Duration	No	The timeline's duration. To edit the duration, trim the clip directly in the timeline window.
Audio Tracks	No	The number of audio tracks in the timeline.
Subtitle Tracks	No	The number of subtitle tracks in the timeline.
Aspect Ratio	Yes	The timeline's aspect ratio.
User Operations	Yes	The permitted operations a user can do while the timeline plays.

Chapter Properties

The Chapter Properties palette shows the current chapter point's attributes.

Table 6-4: **Chapter Properties palette attributes**

PROPERTY	EDITABLE	DESCRIPTION
Name	Yes	The chapter name.
Description	Yes	Informative text for the chapter.
Chapter #	No	The chapter point number.
In	No	The position in time of the chapter point. To edit the In point, move the chapter in the Timeline window.
Poster	Yes	The position in time of the frame representing the chapter point. By default, this is the same as the In point. Poster frames are used for scene selection menus.

Playlist Properties

The Playlist Properties palette is shown when a playlist is selected in the Project tab.

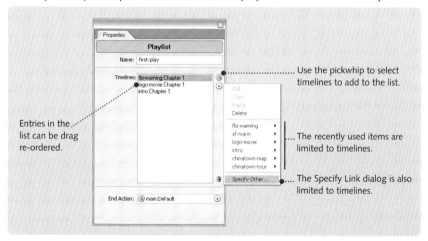

Table 6-5: **Playlist Properties palette attributes**

PROPERTY	EDITABLE	DESCRIPTION
Name	Yes	The playlist name.
Timelines	Yes	The list of timelines to play in sequential order.
End Action	Yes	The destination shown when the playlist finishes. Possible attributes are in the form of menu:button, timeline:chapter point, playlist, or Not Set.

Disc Properties

The Disc Properties palette is shown when the Project tab is current and anything other than a menu or timeline is selected, including when there is no selection.

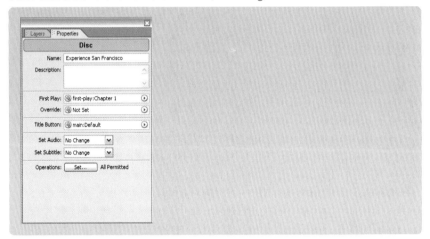

Figure 6-28: **Disc Properties palette**

Table 6-6: **Disc Properties palette attributes**

PROPERTY	EDITABLE	DESCRIPTION
Name	Yes	The disc name shown on a computer. Limited to 31 characters.
Description	Yes	Informative text for the disc.
First Play	Yes	The first menu or timeline shown when the disc begins to play.
Override	Yes/No	Replaces the End Action property of the disc's first play. Possible attributes are in the form of menu:button, timeline:chapter point, playlist, or Not Set. This is not editable when the first play has not been set.
Title Button	Yes	The link shown when the Title key is pressed on a remote control.
Set Audio	Yes	The default audio track for the disc.
Set Subtitle	Yes	The default subtitle track for the disc.
User Operations	Yes	The permitted operations a user can do while the disc plays.

User Operations

User Operations (UOPs) are the interactions a viewer has with the DVD. These operations are accessed with a DVD remote control with a settop box, or with the mouse pointer in a software based DVD player. A user operation can represent a single operation or a collection of similar operations. A common example is disabling all user operations to prevent fast forwarding through the FBI warning video. Encore DVD has three User Operations dialogs, one for a menu, a timeline, or the disc.

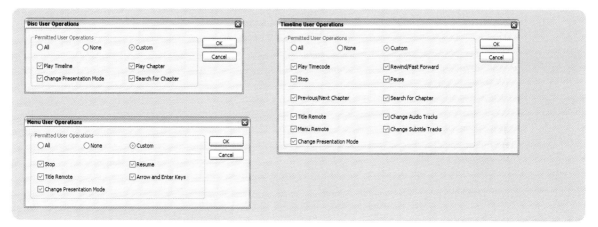

Figure 6-29: **Menu, timeline, and disc user operations**

 To see a explanation for a user operation, mouse over the text and a tool tip will appear.

ACCESSING USER OPERATIONS

*   To set user operations for a menu, click Set in the menu's Properties palette or choose Menu > Set Menu User Operations.

*   To set user operations for a timeline, click Set in the timeline's Properties palette or choose Timeline > Set Timeline User Operations.

*   To set user operations for the disc, click Set in the Disc's Properties palette or choose File > Set Disc User Operations.

Character Palette

Use the Character palette to set text properties. Select a range of text, or an entire text block, and choose from the options in the palette. Although the options are not as extensive as the option in Photoshop, Encore DVD's text options will suffice for the majority of most text formatting needs (Figure 4-9).

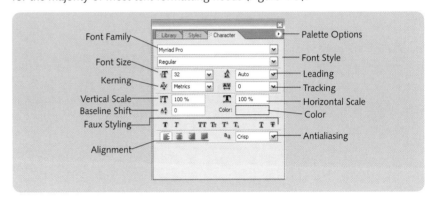

Figure 6-30: **Encore DVD Character palette**

Character Palette Settings

Font Family: All the currently installed fonts.

Font Style: All available styles for a font family.

Font Size: The size of the text.

Leading: The vertical space between baselines of text.

Kerning: The space between two characters.

Tracking: The spacing between all characters in a word or a block of type.

Vertical Scale: The vertical scale of the text.

Horizontal Scale: The horizontal scale of the text.

Baseline Shift: Offset of the text from the baseline.

Color: Color for the selected text.

Faux Styling: Bold, italic, all caps, small caps, superscript, subscript, underline, and strike through styles, respectively, are set here.

Alignment: Controls how lines of text are arranged in paragraphs.

Antialiasing: Sets the smoothness for the text.

Library Palette

The Library palette (Figure 6-31) stores buttons, menus, shapes, text, layer sets, and images. Encore DVD ships with a number of sets of items in the Library palette, but you are free to remove these items and add your own.

To narrow the display of items in the Library palette, click on the filter buttons above the list of library items. The items that are filtered out are temporarily hidden.

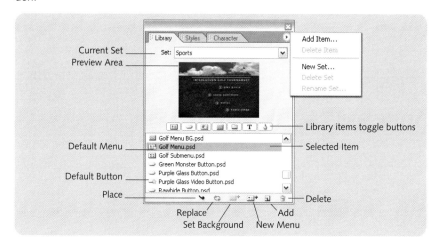

Figure 6-31: **The Library palette**

Adding Buttons and Creating Menus
You can add items to a menu by clicking the Place button, ✈ . It places the selected button or image from the Library palette onto the current menu. The Replace button, ↻ , swaps a selected button or layer from the current menu with the selected item in the Library palette. You can also drag a button or an image from the Library palette to a menu. The New Menu button, ▣⁺ , creates a new menu from the selected menu.

Importing Items
To add items to the current Library set, do one of the following.

Supported formats are listed in Table 6-1 on page 125.

- Drag buttons or menus to the palette.

- Click the Add button, ⬕ , at the bottom of the palette.

- Right-click inside the list and chose New Item.

- Click the fly-out button, ⊙ , and choose Add Item.

Creating Sets
Sets are a collection of Library Items. Encore DVD includes several default Library sets, but you can create, rename, and delete your own sets using the palette's fly-out menu.

The Styles palette works the same way too.

Setting the Default Menu and Button

If you use a menu or button a lot, you can set the default menu and button by right-clicking on a button or menu and choosing Set as Default Button or Set as Default Menu from the contextual menu.

Styles Palette

All style files are a Photoshop file with a single layer containing one or more layer effects.

The Styles palette contains graphic effects for embellishing menus. There are three categories of Styles: text, shape, and image.

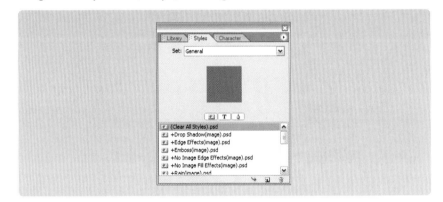

Figure 6-32: **Styles palette**

A text, shape, or image style can be applied to any single layer, regardless of layer type. When a style is applied to a layer set, however, only certain layers within the layer set will be affected by the style.

- When applied to a layer set, a text style is applied to the first text layer in the layer set that is not a highlight layer.

- When applied to a layer set, a shape style is applied to the first shape layer in the layer set that is not a highlight layer.

- When applied to a layer set, an image style is applied to all layers in the layer set, except highlight layers.

To apply a style do one of the following.

- Drag a style from the Styles palette onto an item in the Menu Editor window.

- Select an item in the Menu Editor or Layers palette, and double-click a style in the Styles palette.

To remove a style apply the style named "Clear All Styles.psd."

When you apply a text or shape style on an item with existing styles, the old style
is removed and the new style is applied. Image styles, however, are additive. If you
apply an image style to a layer that already has a style, the existing style remains
and the image style is added. If an image style is applied to a layer with a style that
has the same layer effects as the image style being applied, the layer favors the
newly applied image style.

Layers Palette

Encore DVD has a Layers palette for inspecting, hiding and locking layers and for
converting layers to buttons. It resembles the Photoshop Layers palette but is a little different (Figure 4-8).

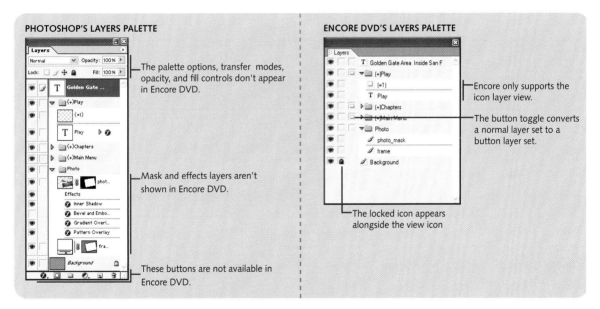

Figure 6-33: **Comparing Layers palettes between Photoshop and Encore DVD**

Moving Layers
The Layers palette in Encore DVD unfortunately does not support direct manipula-
tion of layer order like the Photoshop Layers palette. This means you cannot pick
up a layer with the cursor and drag it to a new location in the palette. Instead, you
have to use the keyboard shortcuts to move layers and layer sets.

Table 6-7: **Layers palette commands**

FUNCTION	MENU COMMAND & SHORTCUT
Move layer to the top of a layer set, or a layer set to the top of the stacking order.	• Object > Arrange > Bring to Front • Shift+Ctrl+]
Move layer up one level within a layer set, or a layer set up one level in the stacking order.	• Object > Arrange > Bring Forward • Ctrl+]
Move layer down one level within a layer set, or a layer set down one level in the stacking order.	• Object > Arrange > Send Back • Ctrl+[
Move layer to the bottom of a layer set, or a layer set to the bottom of the stacking order.	• Object > Arrange > Send to Back • Shift+Ctrl+[

Timeline and Monitor Windows

TIMELINE WINDOW

A timeline is a "container" for assembling video, audio, and subtitles into a single DVD-Video disc. In the timeline, you set the language code for audio and subtitle tracks, and you add chapter points in the video track. Timelines are internal to the Encore DVD project file and are not saved externally. The maximum number of timelines in a Encore DVD project is 99.

Timelines appear in the Project and Timelines tabs. When a timeline is opened for editing, it appears in a Timeline window. When multiple timelines are open in the same window, they appear as separate tabs. A tab can be torn off to create a new Timeline window, or it can be dragged into the tab area of another Timeline window to be docked within it.

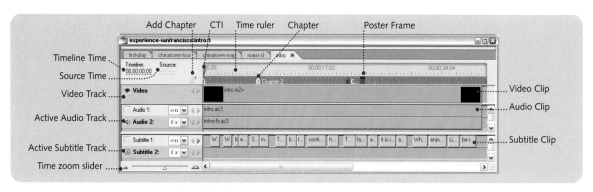

Figure 6-34: **Timeline window**

Although Encore DVD's timeline window might look a like a nonlinear editor (NLE), it is *not* an NLE—it has crude editing functions and is limited to one video and audio clip per track, and timelines cannot be nested. Also, note that the multiple tracks do not equate to a multitrack editor. Each track represents a single audio source that may be stereo or surround sound. Use an NLE for sophisticated edits and for combining more than one video clip into a single file to be imported into Encore DVD.

Multiple still images are, however, allowed in a video track.

The timeline's editing timebase is 29.97 frames per second (fps) for NTSC projects and 25 fps for PAL projects. It is the frame rate and reference scale in time for clips and chapter points. A timeline's duration is determined by the time span of the clips embedded within it, including any empty space at the start or between clips, but not any empty space at the end of the last clip. As clips are added at the end, the timeline's duration grows, and as clips are removed at the end, the duration shrinks.

The maximum duration for a timeline is 9;59;59;29 for NTSC and 9;59;59;29 for PAL.

 While Encore DVD supports only one video track, it supports up to 8 audio tracks and up to 32 subtitle tracks.

Monitor Window

The Monitor window shows video for the current timeline and has controls for playing and stopping playback, adding chapter points, and adding and editing subtitles. Unlike the Project Preview window, which previews the project, the Monitor window is for viewing timelines only.

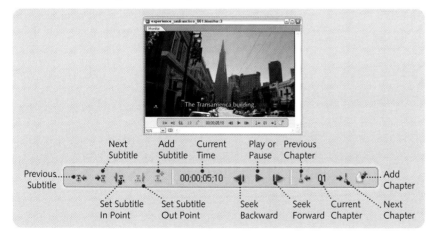

Figure 6-35: **Monitor window**

Creating Timelines and Placing Video, Audio, and Stills

To add video or an image to a timeline, open the Project tab and do one of the following.

- Choose the video or one still image in the Project window, and choose Timeline > New Timeline. Encore DVD creates a timeline with the video or image in the video track. If more than one still is selected, a wizard will appear asking for a common still duration.

- Choose Timeline > New Timeline. Drag a video or images from the Project tab to the video track. Encore DVD places the video at the beginning of the timeline, regardless of where in the timeline you release the mouse. It places images wherever you drop them, and adds a chapter at the image's In point.

 If you create a new timeline from a video asset and multiple audio assets, Encore DVD automatically creates additional tracks for the audio.

TRIMMING

Subtitle and image clips, however, do allow for gaps between clips.

Video and audio clips are trimmed in the Timeline window. Place the cursor near the beginning (head) or end (tail) of the clip and click-drag the edge of the clip to trim. Because video clips must start at time zero, when you trim video, the In point remains at time zero while the clip's tail is shortened.

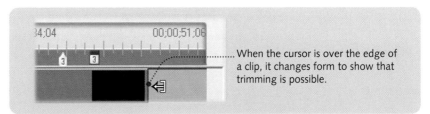

Figure 6-36: **Trimming clips**

SETTING LANGUAGES

To set the language for an audio or subtitle track, select a language from the drop down menu to the right of the track name.

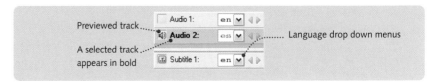

Figure 6-37: **Setting languages for a track**

CREATING CHAPTER POINTS

To add a chapter point, move the Current Time Indicator (CTI) to the desired location and choose Timeline > Add Chapter, press the * on the numeric keypad, or press Ctrl+F1. You can also right-click on the timeline ruler and choose Add Chapter from the contextual menu.

To show the names for chapters in the time ruler, press Ctrl+8, or choose View> Show Chapter Names.

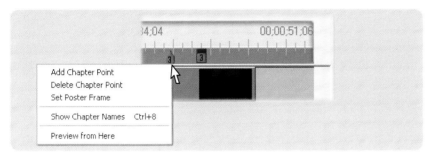

Figure 6-38: **Setting chapters with the contextual menu**

Chapter points can be edited by dragging them to a new location. Each timeline has a chapter 1 at time zero that cannot be edited or moved because of the DVD specification.

SETTING THE POSTER FRAME

The poster frame for a chapter defaults to the same frame location as the chapter. You set the poster frame by selecting the chapter and choosing Timeline > Set Poster Frame or pressing Shift+Ctrl+F1.

Poster frames tend to occur after the Chapter.

 The location for a poster frames can be edited in the Properties palette, or by pressing Ctrl and Alt while dragging the chapter point.

The best example of setting a poster frame is when you have a timeline with several scenes and fades to black in between. Most likely, you would set the chapters in the black, but the posters would be a frame from each scene. The poster frame is important because when you create video thumbnail buttons on a menu, the layer marked for video uses the poster frame.

Layers marked for video are prefixed with a percentage sign inside parentheses (%).

IMPORTING CHAPTERS FROM ADOBE PREMIERE PRO

A sequence marker in Premiere Pro can be set as a chapter point for use in Encore DVD. With Premiere Pro 1.5, chapter markers can be embedded in MPEG-2 and AVI files.

To add markers in Premiere Pro that are readable in Encore DVD follow these steps (Refer to Figure 6-39 on page 164).

1. Open the Program view or Timeline window. Move the CTI to a relevant time requiring a chapter marker.

2. Choose Marker > Set Sequence Marker > Unnumbered or press * on the numeric keypad.

3. Double-click the marker in the timeline ruler. The Marker dialog appears. In the Marker dialog, enter a name for the chapter in the Chapter field and click OK.

Repeat steps 1 through 5 until all chapter markers are created.

4. Select the sequence in the Project window and choose File > Export > Adobe Media Encoder. Choose "MPEG2-DVD" from the format drop down menu. Choose a transcoding preset that matches the video format and your video quality needs and click OK and save the resulting file.

5. Import the file into Encore DVD and create a timeline from it by selecting the file and choosing Timeline > New Timeline or press Ctrl+T with the file selected.

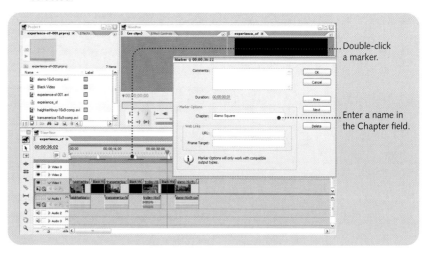

Figure 6-39: **Importing markers from Premiere Pro**

 Encore DVD has rules regarding the proximity of chapters to ensure compliance with the DVD specification. When creating chapter points, place them at least 15 frames apart because Encore DVD will move chapter points that do not follow this rule.

Workspaces

A workspace is a saved arrangement of palettes and windows. A workspace records which palettes and windows are open and records their size and location. You create a workspace to tailor the screen layout for specific workflows and tasks. For example, Encore DVD has preset workspaces for menu design, timeline editing, and link and properties inspection, but you can create your own.

To choose a workspace, select one from the Window > Workspace submenu. You delete workspaces from the Window > Workspace submenu. To create a workspace.

1. Open, position, and scale the windows and palettes for the workspace. Close windows and palettes that are not needed.

2. Choose Window > Workspace > Save Workspace.

3. Enter a name for the workspace, and click Save.

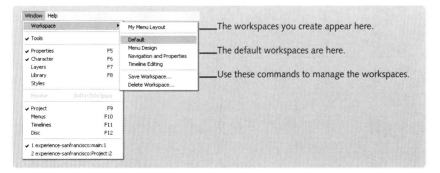

Figure 6-40: **Workspaces submenu**

Project Preview Window

The Project Preview window provides both a video area and the remote control functions for proofing a project. To display the Preview window, choose File > Project Preview, or press Ctrl+Alt+Space. You can also initiate preview by right-clicking on a menu or timeline in the Project tab and choosing Preview from Here.

Preview from Here is also available in the Menu Editor's contextual menu and in the Timeline's time ruler contextual menu.

Figure 6-41: **Preview window**

Project Preview Controls

Render Motion: Renders a motion menu.

Zoom level: The size of the monitor area.

Audio: The drop down menu shows the current audio track and language.

Subtitles: Toggles the subtitle display on or off. The drop-down menu shows the current subtitle track and language.

Up, Left, Enter, Right, and Down arrow keys: Select buttons on a menu. The Enter button activates the selected button.

Transport controls: Previous chapter, Stop, Pause, Play, Next Chapter.

Menu: Shows the menu specified by the timeline's Remote Control Menu Button property.

Title: Shows the disc's Title Button link.

 # Field and Enter: Enter a chapter number or button number and click the Arrow button to the right of the field.

Execute End Action: Engages the timeline's or menu's end action.

Exit Here: Exits the preview and displays the timeline or menu last previewed.

Exit and Return: Exits preview and returns to the place where preview began.

KEYBOARD SHORTCUTS

The Project Preview window has the following keyboard shortcuts.

Table 6-8: **Preview window keyboard shortcuts**

FUNCTION	SHORTCUT
Select a button on a menu.	Number keys (1-9)
Activate a currently selected button.	Enter key
Navigation controls	Up, Down, Left, or Right Arrow
Go to the disc's remote control title link	Home
Go to a timeline's remote control menu link	Insert
Execute the current end action	End Key
Play/Pause	Space bar
Go to the next chapter	Ctrl+Right Arrow
Go to the previous chapter	Ctrl+Left Arrow

Reading the Status Area

The status area shows information regarding the current menu or timeline, time, button, or chapter, as well as the audio format (PCM or Dolby Digital) and the render or transcode status (Figure 6-42).

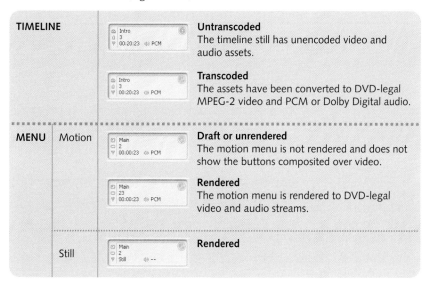

Figure 6-42: **Status area**

Preparing Still Menus

This chapter covers the creation of still menus in Photoshop and Encore DVD, the integration between the two applications, and how to set links in Encore DVD.

For more information on the characteristics of a still menu, see "Still Menu" on page 33.

The Workflow

Encore DVD has two workflows for creating still menus: working exclusively in Encore DVD or designing menus in Photoshop before importing them to Encore DVD. Figure 7-1 shows the workflow for creating menus in either application. Table 7-3 lists Encore DVD's Photoshop support.

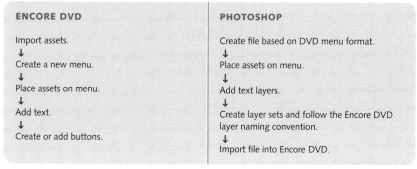

ENCORE DVD	PHOTOSHOP
Import assets.	Create file based on DVD menu format.
↓	↓
Create a new menu.	Place assets on menu.
↓	↓
Place assets on menu.	Add text layers.
↓	↓
Add text.	Create layer sets and follow the Encore DVD layer naming convention.
↓	↓
Create or add buttons.	Import file into Encore DVD.

Figure 7-1: **The two still menu creation workflows**

Working in Photoshop

Encore DVD uses the Photoshop file format (.PSD) for menus. For this reason, use Encore to create menus because it correctly renders Photoshop layers, layer sets, and layer effects. Text editing, moving, and scaling are also supported in Encore DVD. Moving back and forth between the two applications is easy and changes made in one appear immediately in the other.

Preparing Images

Before importing a layered Photoshop file into Encore DVD, do the following.

1. Size the document according to both the project's TV standard and the desired aspect ratio.

2. Create the design and organize the layers according to the Encore DVD layer set naming convention. Place layers associated with one button into a single layer set with a unique name. Duplicate names could confuse you when creating links.

3. Save the file as a Photoshop file (.PSD). Select File > Save or press Ctrl+S.

4. In Encore DVD, use File > Import as Menu or press Shift+Ctrl+I to import it.

CREATING A PHOTOSHOP FILE FOR A DVD MENU

The first step is to choose the correct size for the menu and the project.

1. Open Photoshop. Choose File > New... (Ctrl+N).

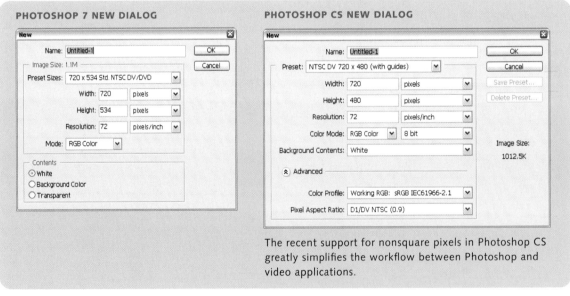

The recent support for nonsquare pixels in Photoshop CS greatly simplifies the workflow between Photoshop and video applications.

Figure 7-2: **Differences between the Photoshop 7 and Photoshop CS New dialogs**

2. In the New dialog, choose a preset that reflects the project's television standard and the menu's aspect ratio. Table 7-1 lists the presets available in Photoshop 7 and Photoshop CS.

Table 7-1: **New file presets for DVD in Photoshop 7 and Photoshop CS**

PHOTOSHOP 7 PRESET	PHOTOSHOP CS PRESET
720 x 534 Std. NTSC DV/DVD	NTSC DV, 720 x 480
864 x 480 Widescreen NTSC DV/DVD	NTSC Widescreen, 720 x 480
768 x 576 PAL Std. PAL	PAL D1/DV, 720 x 576
1024 x 576 Wide PAL	PAL D1/DV Widescreen, 720 x 576

3. Name the file, choose RGB for the color mode, and click OK.

 To create a full-frame image for a menu background or for an image in a timeline slide show, follow these same size requirements.

Encore DVD Layer Naming Convention

Other workflows prohibit making changes to a menu because they use flattened images or they do not allow you to move or edit layers. Encore DVD, by contrast, can edit the most common attributes of layers, such as position and text.

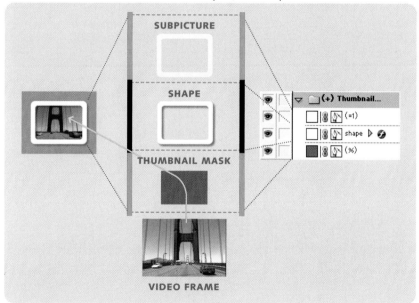

Figure 7-3: **Structure of a Photoshop menu**

Encore DVD uses Photoshop layer sets for buttons and has a naming convention as shown in Table 7-2. Figure 7-3 shows a portion of a layered Photoshop file that follows the convention. This convention enables Encore DVD to:

- recognize buttons automatically when they are imported

- move and scale all layers associated with a button simultaneously

- calculate the highlight region from the layer set's physical area.

Table 7-2: **Encore DVD layer naming convention**

MENU ITEM	PHOTOSHOP ITEM	PREFIX EXAMPLE
Button	Layer set	(+) Play button
Button highlight (subpicture)	A single text, image, or shape layer that uses only one color. A button can have up to three individual highlights.	(=1) Bullet (=2) Underline (=3) Text overlay
Video thumbnail mask	Any layer	(%) Thumbnail mask

Keep the following in mind when preparing layers in Photoshop.

- Regular layers or layer sets do not need a special prefix.

- The (=1), (=2), and (=3) subpicture layers map to the Color 1, Color 2, and Color 3 properties in a menu color set.

- The (%) layer for video thumbnails is surprisingly powerful for compositing video thumbnails on a menu. For instance, Encore DVD supports transparency.

- Although Photoshop 7 introduced layer support for TIFF files, Encore DVD requires that layered files be in Photoshop (*.psd*) format.

LIMITATIONS OF PHOTOSHOP SUPPORT IN ENCORE DVD

Encore DVD has technology borrowed from Photoshop to create menus, and it renders Photoshop files faithfully, but Encore DVD does not support all layer attributes in its user interface—it is not meant as a replacement for Photoshop, but as an extension. If you need to edit one of these features, do not worry. You can easily edit the menu in Photoshop and see the changes reflected in Encore DVD immediately by choosing Edit > Edit in Photoshop, pressing Shift+Ctrl+M, or clicking the Edit in Photoshop button, , in the Tool palette. Table 7-3 lists Encore DVD's limitations and corresponding work around.

Table 7-3: **Limitations in Encore DVD for Photoshop 7 and CS file support**

FEATURE	CAVEATS
Layer structure	Dragging layers and layer sets is not supported in the Encore DVD Layers palette.
	Work around: Use Cut, Copy, and Paste or one of the menu commands in Object > Arrange.
	Layer thumbnails are not shown.
	Work around: Rely on names and layer set organization.
Positioning items	Items cannot be rotated or skewed.
	Work around: Rotate or skew items in Photoshop.
	No grids in Encore DVD.
	Work around: Use Photoshop's grids or use guides in Encore DVD.
Text	Encore DVD preserves text with hyphenation or OpenType features, but these settings cannot be changed in Encore DVD.
	Work around: Set OpenType features and spellcheck in Photoshop.
	Photoshop CS has a new feature to place text inside a shape layer or on a path.
	Work around: The text can be edited in Encore DVD, but not the shape.
Layer effects	Encore DVD renders layer effects, but the Drop Shadow layer effect is the only one modifiable in Encore DVD.
	Work around: Add Styles in Encore DVD, but edit layer effects in Photoshop.
16-bit images	Photoshop introduces support for 16-bit layers, and Encore only supports 8-bit layers.
	Work around: Convert images to 8 bits by choosing Image > Mode > 16 bits/Channel.

An Overview of the Tutorials in this Chapter

The tutorials in this chapter return to the idea presented in Chapter 3—creating a DVD for tourists visiting San Francisco. Figure 7-4 is a flowchart for the project, and a star indicates which menus are created in the tutorials.

The disc's first play is a playlist containing a FBI warning movie and an animation for my fictitious production company, Spin Films. When it finishes, it links to the disc's main menu. The main menu links to an introductory video on San Francisco, a Credits menu, a Help menu, and lastly a Sites menu. The sites contains links to sub menus for a few neighborhoods in San Francisco. This chapter and the next one will use variations of this project for the book's tutorials.

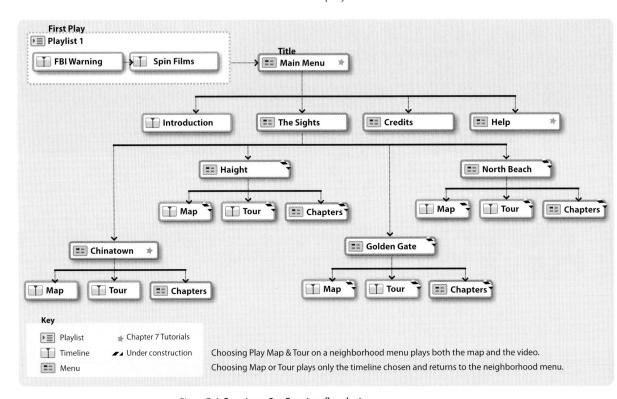

Figure 7-4: **Experience San Francisco flowchart**

Working in Photoshop

Tutorial 1: Create a Button
In this tutorial, I show you how to add buttons to an existing Photoshop file. You'll create a button, create text, add a subpicture highlight, and name them using the Encore naming convention.

 Copy the Tutorial 1 *folder from the* Tutorials *folder on the DVD-ROM to your hard drive.*

1. Launch Photoshop and open file named *main.psd,* which is shown below.   *Press Ctrl+O to open a file.*

BEFORE (menu.psd)

AFTER (main_complete.psd)

In this chapter, we will add buttons to this menu in Photoshop and import the menu into Encore DVD where we will make small edits.

2. Choose View > Show > Guides (Ctrl+;). These guides match the safe area guides in Encore DVD. You will place the buttons within the safe area's bounds.   *The safe areas are the inner 80% (title) and 90% (action) of the video image.*

3. Open the Layers palette (choose Window > Layers if it is hidden). This palette will reflect the changes made to the structure of the Photoshop file.

4. Select the Text tool, T , in the Tool palette. The text tool, as its name implies, creates text layers on the Photoshop canvas. You will use it to create the text buttons on the menu.   *Press T to switch to the Text tool.*

5. Open the Character palette (Window > Character) and select the following text properties.

   – Choose Myriad Pro for the font family and Semibold Italic for the font style. These fonts ship with Encore DVD, but if they're not on your system, Arial will suffice.

   – Set the text size to 24 point.

   – Set the text color to white. To do this, click the color swatch and in the Color Picker dialog, enter 255 in the R, G, and B edit fields. Click OK.

   – With the Text tool, click in the area below the title and enter "Welcome." Position the text so it aligns with the words Main Menu and San Francisco.

To switch to the Rectangle tool, press U. Press Shift+U repeatedly if another shape tool is current.

6. It's time to create the subpicture for this button. Select the Rectangle tool, ☐ , in the Tool palette. This tool will create a Photoshop shape layer that will serve as the Play button's highlight.

 – Using the Rectangle tool, draw a rectangle to the left of the text. Next, go to the Layers palette and double-click the shape layer's fill color. Pick a yellow color with the Color Picker dialog.

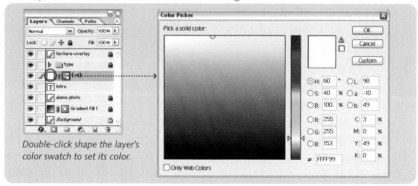

Double-click shape the layer's color swatch to set its color.

7. For the rectangle to function as a highlight, give its layer name the subpicture prefix from the Encore layer naming convention.

 – Select the shape layer in the Layer palette, press Enter, and type "(=1) underline highlight" over the existing name.

8. The text and shape layers must now become a button.

 – With the (=1) layer selected, link the two buttons together by clicking the link icon for the text layer.

 – Move these into a layer set by choosing Layer > New > Layer Set from Linked. In the New Set from Linked dialog, type "(+) Intro" in the field for the button name and click OK.

 – The layer set is now a button layer set.

Tutorial 2: Add Buttons

Now that you have created a single button, it is easy to copy this button, change its position and the text, and make another button from it.

1. Select the (+) Intro layer set and right-click on the name (clicking on the folder icon will display different options). Choose Duplicate Layer Set... from the contextual menu.

Or choose Layer > Duplicate Layer Set...

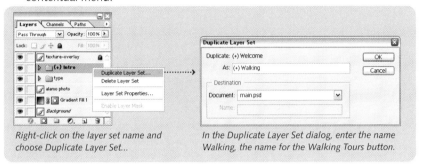

Right-click on the layer set name and choose Duplicate Layer Set...

In the Duplicate Layer Set dialog, enter the name Walking, the name for the Walking Tours button.

2. In the Duplicate Layer Set dialog, change the layer set's name to "(+) The Sights" and click OK.

3. With the layer set selected, switch to the Move Layer tool, ⯈⊕ . Hold Shift and Press the Down arrow five times, or a total of 50 pixels. Holding Shift moves the button 10 pixels each time you press the Down arrow.

Pressing V switches to the Move Layer tool.

4. Choose the Text tool and change the word Play to "The Sights."

5. Repeat steps 2 through 4, but create a Help button from the The Sights button.

6. Repeat steps 2 through 4 again, but create a Credits button from the Help button. The menu should look like the following menu.

7. Save the file. Choose File > Save or press Ctrl+S.

Working in Encore DVD

You can import menus from Photoshop and make small edits in Encore DVD. Use Encore the DVD Library palette to make a menu, or create a menu from scratch from imported assets. Tutorials 3 through 5 cover these scenarios.

 Copy the Tutorial 3 *folder from the* Tutorials *folder on the DVD-ROM to your hard drive.*

Tutorial 3: Import a Menu

Now that the menu has been designed, you'll add it to a project and integrate it with other content into the project.

1.   Launch Encore DVD and open the *Experience San Francisco* project file from the Tutorial 3 folder.

Press Shift+Ctrl+I to import a Photoshop file as a menu.

2.   Choose File > Import as Menu… and choose the *Main.psd* file that you completed in the previous tutorial.

3.   The menu opens in a Menu Editor window.

4.   Save the project. Choose File > Save or press Ctrl+S.

How Encore DVD Works with Photoshop Files

Import versus Import as Menu

File > Import interprets a Photoshop file as flattened assets. Only use File > Import for images that are parts of a menu and not a complete menu. You also use File > Import for video and audio files.

To properly import a Photoshop file as a menu, use File > Import as Menu and not File > Import. Import as Menu correctly interprets a Photoshop file's layer sets into a DVD menu.

If you unintentionally make this mistake, simply clear the file from the project (Edit > Clear or press the Delete key) and reimport the Photoshop file using File > Import as Menu.

Copying versus Linking to the Original

When Encore DVD imports a Photoshop file as a menu, it does not link to the original Photoshop file. Rather, it places a copy of it in the project folder.

Tutorial 4: Make Changes to an Existing Menu

Assume you need to change the text for the Credits button to make it an About button. With the use of Encore DVD's Text tool, this tutorial shows you how to make this simple change.

1.   Open the Main menu if it is not open.

2. Select the Horizontal Text tool, T , from the Tool palette. Click and type "About" over the word "Credits."

You should also rename the Credits menu. Select it in the Project tab and choose Edit > Rename.

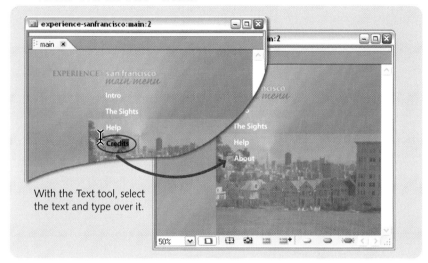

With the Text tool, select the text and type over it.

3. Save the project. Choose File > Save or press Ctrl+S.

Tutorial 5: Use the Library Palette

In this tutorial, you will create a Help menu entirely in Encore DVD with the Library palette, imported assets, Copy and Paste, and the Text tool.

For a quick overview on the Library palette, see page 156.

1. Choose Window > Library. Choose New Set from the Library palette's fly-out menu. Enter "SF DVD" for the name. Click OK.

2. Click the New Item button, ⬚, at the bottom of the Library palette.

    – An Open dialog appears. In the Tutorial 5 folder, select the file *menu-background.psd.*

Click the New Item button   Select the file *menu-background.psd*   Click Open

    – The file is added to the Library palette as a menu. It can now be used in this project or any other project you create.

3. In the Library palette, select the file and click the New Menu button, 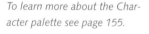, at the bottom of the Library palette.

4. In the Project tab, select the newly created menu, and rename it Help by choosing Edit > Rename.

5. Open the Photos folder and drag the photo "trolley" to the Menu Editor window. Position the photo along the bottom edge of the menu.

6. Open the Chinatown menu, select the Main Menu button, and choose Edit > Copy or press Ctrl+C.

7. Switch back to the Help menu and choose Edit > Paste or press Ctrl+V.

    – A copy of the button is placed on the menu. Notice how Encore DVD remembers the location of the previous button and places the pasted button in the same place.

8. Now you need to add the Help menu text. Launch a text editor. I prefer Notepad in this instance. Open the file *help-text.txt*, which is in the Tutorial 5 folder.

9. Select all the text in the document by pressing Ctrl+A and then copy it by choosing Edit > Copy or pressing Ctrl+C.

10. Switch to Encore DVD and open the Help menu.

To learn more about the Char-
acter palette see page 155.

11. Switch to the Text Tool, click on the menu, and choose Edit > Paste or press Ctrl+V. The text is pasted on the menu. Select all the text again and change its type properties to Myriad Pro Regular, 24 for the size, and 36 for the leading, and white for the fill color.

12. Position the text so its left margin aligns with the San Francisco text and is in between the title text and the Main Menu button.

13. Finish this menu by adding a drop shadow to the text. Select the text layer with the Selection tool, ⬉ , and choose Object > Drop Shadow or press Shift+Ctrl+O. Set the settings as they appear in the following dialog box and click OK.

14. The final Help menu should look something like this.

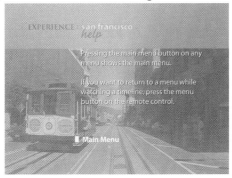

Setting Button Properties and Links

Tutorials 6 through 10 cover setting button properties such as button numbering and routing. It also covers the creation of links and overrides for buttons, as well as setting the First Play and Title Remote button properties.

Tutorial 6: Edit the Routing and Numbering

It is time to inspect the button numbering and routing on the Main menu and to make slight adjustments to both.

To learn more about button routing, see page 17. To learn more about button numbering, see page 19.

1. Open the Main menu. Display the routing and button numbers by choosing View > Show Routing or pressing Ctrl+7. You can also turn on this display by pressing the Show Routing button, ⊞, at the bottom of the Menu Editor window.

2. When the routing is displayed, a border with four arrows and a square are drawn over each button.

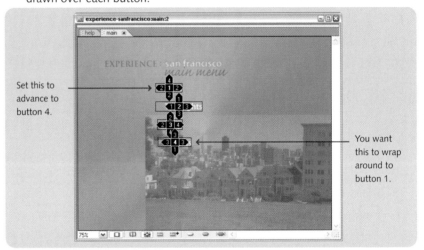

Set this to advance to button 4.

You want this to wrap around to button 1.

3. The square in the middle of the button is the button's number. The arrows correspond to the buttons that will be selected by pressing the arrow keys on a remote control.

   – When you place the cursor over one of the arrow keys, you see a prohibited cursor ⊘. This cursor appears because the menu is set to use automatic routing by default.

4. First, renumber the buttons.

   – Select the Intro button, which is set to 3.

To view the Properties palette, choose Window > Properties or press F5.

   – In the Properties palette, choose 1 from the number drop-down menu. The Play button changes to 1 and the Main Menu button changes to 3. Whenever you change a button's number, it switches numbers with the button that had the number originally.

5. Finish by adjusting the routing between buttons. To manually set the routing, you need to Deselect All, so the menu properties are visible, and then uncheck

automatic routing in the menu's Properties palette. To deselect all items, choose Edit > Deselect All or press Shift+Ctrl+A.

6. Notice how the left arrow for the Intro button is set to The Sights button when really it should be going to the About button. Move the pointer to the Intro button's down arrow. Instead of a prohibited cursor, the cursor changes to a hand, 🖑. The hand represents the ability to manually modify the button routing.

7. Click-drag from the Intro button's left arrow to the About button.

8. Click-drag the right arrow for the About button to the Intro button.

That is it. In the Show Routing mode, it is simple to manually set the button routing. In most cases, automatic routing should suffice, but use manual routing when menus have nonrectangular button layouts.

Tutorial 7: Set Button Links
In this tutorial, you will link the Intro button to the Intro timeline.

1. If the Main menu is not open, open it.

2. Show the Properties palette and also make sure the Project tab is visible.

3. Select the Intro button with the Select tool, ↖ . With the button selected, move the cursor over to the Properties palette and click-drag the pickwhip control, ◉, to the Introduction timeline in the Project tab.

See "Using the Link Control" on page 143 for additional ways to set links.

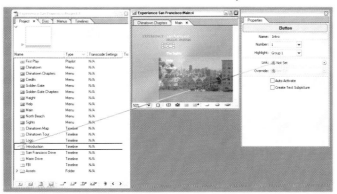

4. The Intro button's Link field is updated to show the link to the Introduction timeline.

5.   Using the same technique, link the The Sights button to The Sights menu, the Help button to the Help menu, and the About button to the About menu.

Tutorial 8: Set the Disc's First Play

The first play is the first menu or timeline shown when the disc begins to play. In this tutorial, you will set user operations, create a playlist, and set the disc's First Play property with the Specify Link dialog.

SET USER OPERATIONS

When you insert a disc and watch the first items on screen, the DVD remote control usually does not work. In this case, the DVD author has disabled the controls on the DVD remote. These controls support user operations.

Hold down the Control key and click both timelines.

1.   Select the FBI and Logo timelines and click the User Operations property Set button in the Properties palette.

2.   In the Timeline User Operations dialog, click the option for None and click OK.

–   The Properties palette will now show that both timelines have their User Operations set to None Permitted.

CREATE A PLAYLIST

When watching a Hollywood DVD title, there are several short movies that play before the disc's main menu appears. For instance, after the FBI warning are a copyright notice, a studio logo animation, or trailers for other movies.

1.   With the FBI and Logo timelines selected, click the New Playlist button, ▦⁺, at the bottom of the Project tab.

- A playlist is created with these two items in the list. If the fbi-warning timeline is at the bottom of the list, move it to the top by click-dragging it above logo-animation.

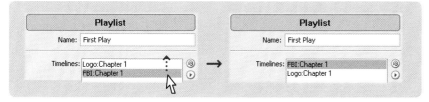

SET THE DISC'S FIRST PLAY

2. Open the Properties palette if it is not already open (Choose Window > Properties or press F5).

3. Show the Disc tab (Window > Disc or press F12). Notice how the Properties palette immediately changes to show the Disc properties. Click the button at the end of the First Play field, ⊙. Choose Specify Other... from the fly-out menu that appears.

4. In the Specify Link dialog, select the playlist you created in Step 1 and click OK.

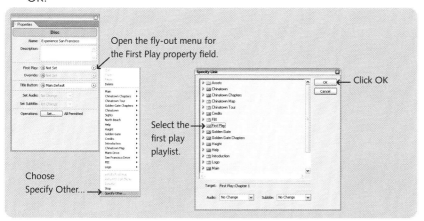

 The fly-out menu only shows the last 20 recently viewed items. If an item doesn't appear in the menu, use the pickwhip or select Specify Other....

Tutorial 9: Setting the Disc's Title Button

The Title Button property is the menu or timeline shown when the viewer presses the Title button on the remote control. It is normally accessible from anywhere on the DVD. For this project, the menu Main will be used for the Title button.

1. With the Disc Properties palette still visible, click the button at the end of the Title Button link field, ⊙. Choose Specify Other... from the fly-out menu that appears.

2. In the Specify Link dialog, select the Main menu and click OK.

Tutorial 10: Setting Button Links with End Actions

For more information on end actions, refer to "End Action" on page 31.

The Chinatown menu has six buttons. The last three buttons already have their link properties set and do not need to be modified. The first three buttons however, have not been set and are the focus of this tutorial. Here, you will set the Map button to play the Chinatown Map timeline and return to the Chinatown menu by overriding the Chinatown Map timeline's end action. See Figure 7-5 for a diagram explaining the navigation.

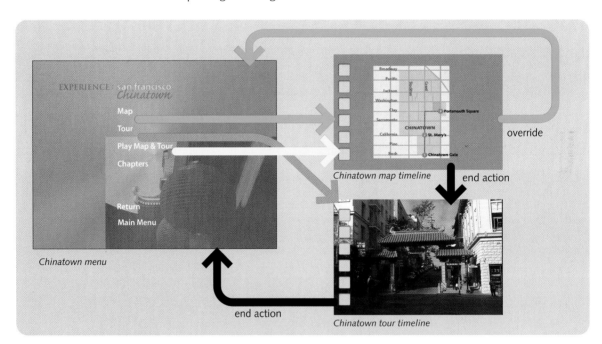

Figure 7-5: **The Chinatown menu**

The Map button links to the Chinatown Map timeline and overrides the timeline's end action by having the DVD player return back to the Chinatown menu. The Chinatown Tour button links to the Chinatown Tour timeline. When it finishes, the DVD player returns to the Chinatown menu.

The Play Map & Tour button links to the Map timeline and does not override it. The result is that it progresses to the Tour timeline.

1. Open the Chinatown menu.

2. Select the Map button and set its Link property to the Chinatown-map timeline.

3. With the Map button still selected, click on the Override fly-out button and choose Link back to Here. This will cause the Map timeline to play, and instead of continuing to the Tour timeline, its assigned end action, it returns to the Chinatown menu.

Photoshop Tips for Customizing Templates

The two most frequent operations performed when customizing templates are changing text and swapping images. Changing text is fairly straightforward, as demonstrated in "Tutorial 4: Making Changes to an Existing Menu"on page 174. However, you can swap images several ways. In the next two tutorials, I cover how to swap images with Crop and Paste Into commands and shape masks.

Tutorial 11: Swapping Images with Paste Into
In this tutorial, you will swap the image of the Palace of Fine Arts on the Slide Show menu for a photograph of Coit tower.

1. Launch Photoshop and open the files *slideshow-11.psd* and *coit-tower.psd,* which are located in the Tutorial 11 folder.

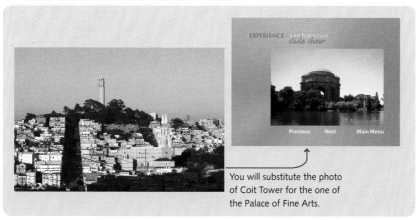

You will substitute the photo of Coit Tower for the one of the Palace of Fine Arts.

2. In the Menu document, select the Palace layer in the Layers palette.

3. Now you need to know the dimensions of this layer. Open the Info palette by choosing Window > Info or pressing F8.

4. Choose Select > Select All or press Ctrl+A. Press the Left arrow key once and then press the Right arrow key to move the layer back.

   – You press the arrow keys to make the selection marquee (or dancing ants, as they are often called) hug the layer's edges so its actual dimensions will appear in the Info palette.

   – Note the size in the Info palette. The Palace layer is 480 x 320 pixels. You need to size the Coit Tower image to this size. Do not discard the selection, you will need it for Step 9.

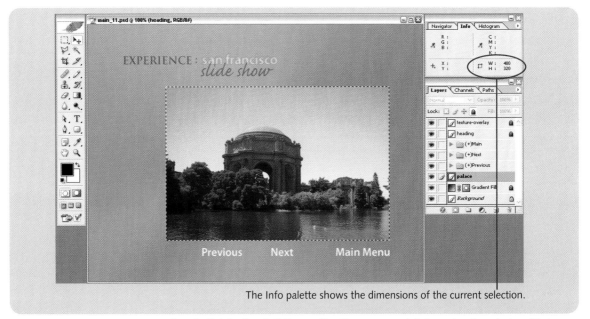

The Info palette shows the dimensions of the current selection.

5. Switch to the Coit Tower file. One approach is to resize the photo with Image > Image Size... and then copy and paste it into the menu template. This approach, however, only works for images that have the same aspect ratio.

If the Options bar is not currently visible, choose Window > Options.

6. Another method that guarantees that the photo will have the correct aspect ratio is to use the Crop tool, ⛏ . Select the Crop tool and enter the following values in the Options bar.

7.   With the Crop tool, click-drag a region over the photo that places more emphasis on the tower.

8.   Finally, crop the image by choosing Image > Crop. Copy the cropped image by choosing Select > Select All and then Edit > Copy.

9.   Switch to the *slideshow-11.psd* file. The Palace layer should still be selected. If it is not, repeat Step 4 only and then choose Edit > Paste Into. This places the Coit Tower image into the document at exactly the same place as the Palace layer.

10. Delete the Palace layer in the Layers palette by single-clicking on the layer and then clicking the Delete Layer button, 🗑, at the bottom of the Layers palette.

Tutorial 12: Reusing Shape Masks

This tutorial shows you how to use guides, the Transform command, and the Marquee tool to place images into the same location as a previous image.

1.   Launch Photoshop and open the files *slideshow-12.psd* and *alamo-square.psd,* which are located in the Tutorial 12 folder.

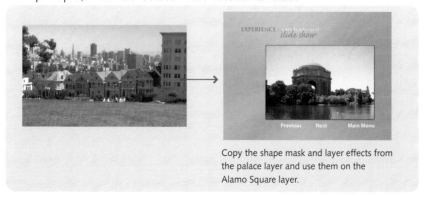

Copy the shape mask and layer effects from the palace layer and use them on the Alamo Square layer.

2. Notice in the slideshow-12 file that the Palace layer has a shape mask and three layer effects.

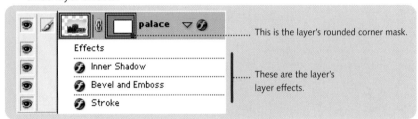

.... This is the layer's rounded corner mask.

.... These are the layer's
layer effects.

3. Switch to the *alamo-square.psd* file and select the Move Layer tool,

   – Click-drag from any point on the image and drag it to the Slideshow_12 window. You will notice the cursor change to the drag-copy cursor, .

4. Switch to the Slideshow_12 document. Move the Alamosquare layer so it is in the same position as the Palace layer.

   – Click the Palace layer in the Layers palette and click again on its shape mask. On the canvas, the layer will refresh to show that its shape mask is selected.

   – Switch to the Direct Selection tool, , drag a marquee around the entire contents of the Palace layer on the canvas, and choose Edit > Copy or press Ctrl+C.

5. Click on the Alamosquare layer and choose Layer > Add Vector Mask. This adds an empty vector mask area to the layer. Choose Edit > Paste or press Ctrl+V to fill the vector mask area with vector information copied from the Palace layer.

   – The shape mask will be now be applied to the Alamosquare layer.

6. Click again on the Palace layer in the Layers palette, then right-click on the layer name and choose Copy Layer Style from the contextual menu.

7. Click on the Alamosquare layer, then right-click on the layer name and choose Paste Layer Style.

– The Alamosquare layer should now match the Palace layer. Feel free to turn off or delete the Palace layer.

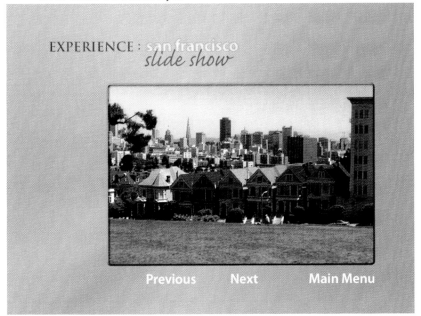

Working with Adobe Illustrator Files

Unfortunately, Encore DVD does not import Illustrator files. If you have a logo in Illustrator, there are two paths to Encore DVD and it is through Illustrator's File > Export command or by opening the file directly in Photoshop. Before I cover these two approaches, however, here is some advice when working with logos.

1. *Always* work with logos in vector form! Most logos are created with drawing tools that generate PostScript—such as Adobe Illustrator or Macromedia Freehand. They are much more flexible than working with a logo that has been saved as a bitmap.

    – Ask the client if they have a corporate identity kit. This usually contains all the logo variations (four-color, two-color, one-color), corporate color specifications, and guidelines indicating how the logo can be used.

2. Does the logo require a typeface to be installed?

    – If yes, make sure you have the typeface installed or the logo will not convert properly in Photoshop.

– Ideally, open the logo in Illustrator and convert all type to outlines by choosing Type > Create Outlines (Shift+Ctrl+O).

 Even though Illustrator offers to embed the typeface to the file, this will not always work if the typeface developer prohibits embedding fonts.

3. In the Illustrator file, is the logo placed on a background?

– If yes, you might want to delete the background in Illustrator if the logo is to be silhouetted in the final design. See Figure 7-6 for examples.

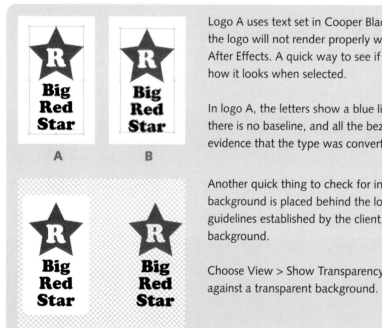

Logo A uses text set in Cooper Black. If Cooper Black is not installed, the logo will not render properly when imported into Photoshop or After Effects. A quick way to see if a logo is using type is to inspect how it looks when selected.

In logo A, the letters show a blue line under the baselines. In logo B, there is no baseline, and all the bezier control points are shown-evidence that the type was converted to outlines.

Another quick thing to check for in Illustrator is whether or not a background is placed behind the logo. Depending on the logo guidelines established by the client, you might be able to remove the background.

Choose View > Show Transparency Grid, which shows the logo against a transparent background.

Figure 7-6: **Working with logos in Adobe Illustrator**

Opening Illustrator Files in Photoshop

You open Illustrator files in Photoshop by rasterizing them. Rasterization converts the vector artwork in the Illustrator file into pixels. To rasterize an Illustrator file with Photoshop, choose File > Open and select the Illustrator file. The Rasterize Generic EPS Format dialog appears.

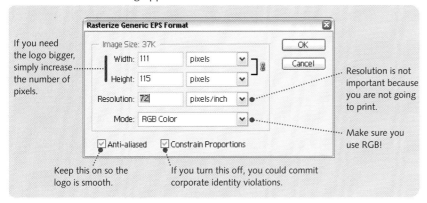

If you need the logo bigger, simply increase the number of pixels.

Resolution is not important because you are not going to print.

Make sure you use RGB!

Keep this on so the logo is smooth.

If you turn this off, you could commit corporate identity violations.

Figure 7-7: **Photoshop's Rasterize Generic EPS Format dialog**

 Make sure to select RGB as the color mode or Encore DVD will not be able to read the file.

Techniques for Automating Production

If you begin to produce DVDs frequently, there will be times when hundreds of images need to be sized to DVD dimensions. You might even want to automate some of the more mundane tasks of naming layers and layer sets according to the Encore DVD naming convention. When this time comes, Photoshop's Actions palette, Batch command, and droplets will meet your needs.

The Actions Palette

An action is a list of Photoshop commands that are performed on one or more files. For instance, an action could create buttons, textures, or properly sized images for DVD menus and timelines. The Actions palette is for recording, editing, playing, and organizing actions. Actions, like layers, can be grouped into sets. Actions can be exported, imported, copied, and deleted.

To view the Actions palette, choose Window > Actions or press or press Alt+F9

 A folder of actions for DVD production is in the Visual Design folder on the DVD-ROM.

To load these actions into Photoshop, follow these steps.

1. Show the Actions palette and choose Load Actions from the palette's fly-out menu.

2. Navigate to theDesign Goodies folder on the DVD, select the actions you want to import, and click OK. Figure 7-8 shows the Actions palette and how to load these palettes into Photoshop.

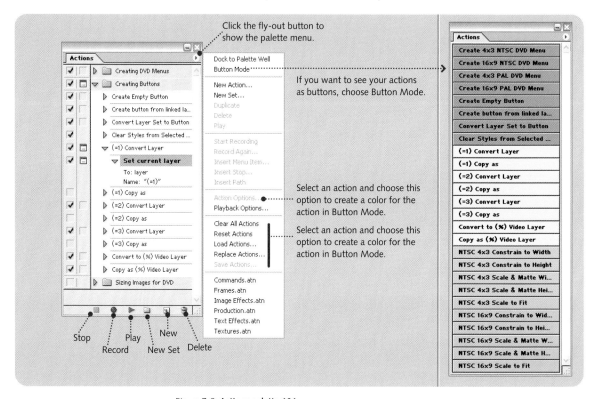

Figure 7-8: **Actions palette 101**

SWITCHING TO BUTTON MODE

I think it was Photoshop 3, but it could have been 2.5.

In early versions of Photoshop, the Actions palette was a palette of one-click buttons to commonly accessed menu commands. Luckily, the Actions palette still has this mode. Choose it from the palette's fly-out menu (Figure 7-8).

The Batch Dialog

Photoshop Actions can also be used for batch processing in the Batch dialog, where you specify an action to perform what files will receive the actions, and a destination and file-naming options for the processed files.

To show the Batch dialog, choose File> Automate> Batch

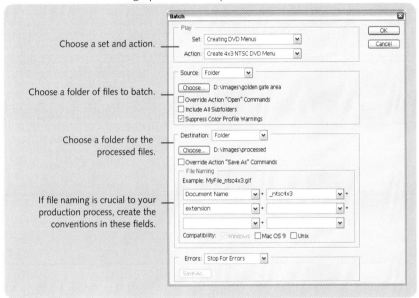

Choose a set and action.

Choose a folder of files to batch.

Choose a folder for the processed files.

If file naming is crucial to your production process, create the conventions in these fields.

Figure 7-9: **The Batch dialog**

Photoshop has four options for choosing source files

- Folder—Pick a folder on the hard drive to process. In most cases, this will be a folder of digital photos or scans. This is probably the best option.

- Import—If you own a scanner that offers integration with Adobe's batch processing, select this option.

- Opened—This processes all the currently opened files in Photoshop. This option is convenient when you have opened all the files prior to batch-processing, but Folder or File Browser is almost always more convenient.

- File Browser—This option processes the selected files in Photoshop's File Browser (Window > File Browser).

Photoshop has three destination options

- None—Alter the files and leave them open.

- Save and Close—Save and close the alterations to the original file.

- Folder—Save altered copies to another location.

Creating Droplets

*To create a droplet, choose
File > Automate > Create Droplet*

Actions can be exported from Photoshop as a droplet, which tells Photoshop how to process files that are dragged onto it. Droplets are most beneficial to the DVD production artist in terms of resizing images to match the television format, NTSC or PAL, and screen aspect ratio, 4:3 or 16:9, being used.

The Create Droplet dialog is similar in appearance to the Batch dialog. The difference is that the Create Droplet dialog lacks the source options because you will be dragging the files to be processed on top of it. Also, the dialog does not do the batch processing but creates the droplet application that does.

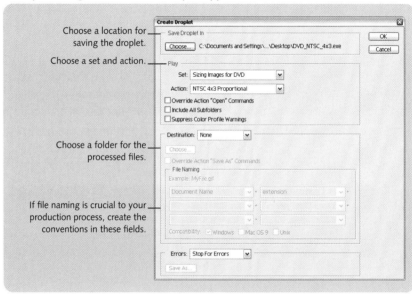

Figure 7-10: **The Create Droplet dialog**

 Keep droplets on the desktop or in an accessible folder if you plan to use them a lot in your workflow. Back your droplets up, too!

Timelines and Motion Menus

In this chapter you will work with timelines and create simple motion motions in Encore DVD.

Timelines

A timeline in Encore DVD is a video title sets (VTS) in DVD specification–speak. More importantly, to the viewers of your DVD, timelines are the video segments they choose to watch when they click a button on a menu. Timelines are easier to create than menus, and the workflow is straightforward, as shown in Figure 8-1.

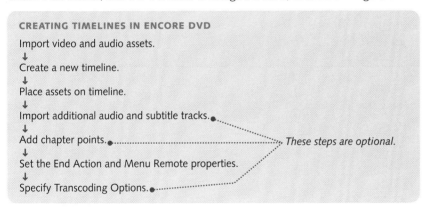

CREATING TIMELINES IN ENCORE DVD

Import video and audio assets.
↓
Create a new timeline.
↓
Place assets on timeline.
↓
Import additional audio and subtitle tracks.
↓
Add chapter points. ·················· *These steps are optional.*
↓
Set the End Action and Menu Remote properties.
↓
Specify Transcoding Options.

Figure 8-1: **Timeline creation workflow**

 Always set the End Action property for timelines and test every timeline's end action in Preview mode. If a timeline has no end action, the disc goes into Stop mode which disorients and inconveniences the viewer.

Embedding Project Links

Why Embed Links?

Embedding project links facilitates integration between Encore DVD and Premiere Pro or After Effects. Selecting an asset and choosing Edit > Edit Original opens the Premiere Pro or After Effects project file. After editing the project and saving a new version of the asset, Encore DVD accepts the changes. If links are not embedded in the asset, Encore DVD cannot edit the original project file.

Embedding a Project Link in Premiere Pro

Select a video or sequence in the Project window and choose File > Export > Movie or press Ctrl+M. In the Export Movie Settings dialog, choose Project in the Embedding Options drop-down list.

Embedding a Project Link in After Effects

After adding a composition to the render queue, click on the composition's Output Module settings. In the Output Module Settings dialog, choose Project Link or Project Link and Copy.

Embedding only a link launches After Effects and loads the project file.

Embedding a link and a copy adds both a link to the original After Effects project file and a copy of it. If the After Effects project is modified and Encore DVD does not receive the updates, embedding a copy gives you the choice to open the modified project or the embedded copy that reflects the asset currently in use in Encore DVD. Should the project go offline, having a copy will also help you to gather any assets that might be needed to recreate the original After Effects project.

Tutorial 13: Import Video and Create Timelines

In this tutorial, you will import a video file and create a timeline from it.

For more information on the Timeline and Monitor windows, see "Timeline and Monitor Windows" on page 151.

1. Copy the Chapter 8 tutorials folder to the hard drive from the Tutorials folder on the DVD. Once the copy is complete, launch Encore DVD.

2. Create a new project by choosing File > New or by pressing Ctrl+N.

3. If the New Project Settings dialog appears, choose NTSC and click OK.

– If you are rarely or never going to create PAL projects, choose NTSC and check the Don't prompt for setting checkbox. All new projects will now be NTSC. Later, should you need to create a PAL project, choose Edit > Preferences > General and check the Prompt for TV Standard checkbox. The New Project Settings dialog will appear, allowing you to choose PAL or NTSC projects.

4. Move the cursor inside the Project tab and right-click below the column headings. Choose Import as Asset from the contextual menu.

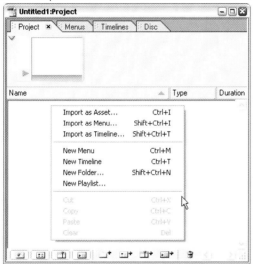

 You can also double-click in the Project tab's list area, choose File > Import, or press Ctrl+I.

5. In the Import as Asset dialog, navigate to where you saved the tutorials for Chapter 8 and open the Tutorial 13 folder. Select the *intro.avi* file, and click Open.

– The *intro.avi* file is added to the Project tab. If you select it, you will see a small thumbnail appear in the preview pane at the top of the Project tab. Preview video and audio assets in the preview area by clicking the Play button, ▶.

6. With the *intro.avi* file selected, click the New Timeline button, ⬚⁺, at the bottom of the Project window.

– Encore DVD creates a timeline from the *avi* asset and automatically places the video and audio streams into the new timeline's tracks .

Anytime is good time to save!

7. Choose File > Save Project and save the project to the Chapter 13 tutorial folder. Name it Tutorial-13 and click OK.

Tutorial 14: Create Chapter Points

Chapter points are time-based locations within a timeline. They are placed where scenes begin or are placed at consistent intervals so viewers can skip through content more quickly and convieniently. In this tutorial, you will add five chapter points to the timeline created in the previous tutorial. I will show you how to add chapter points five different ways!

1. Open the Intro timeline created in Chapter Seven. You open timelines by double-clicking a Timeline icon, 🗐, in the Project tab. Do not confuse the Video Asset File icon, 💻 , with the Timeline icon.

    – The Timeline and Monitor windows open. If for some reason you close the Monitor window, choose Window > Monitor or press Shift+Ctrl+Space.

Or you can choose View > Workspace > Timeline Editing.

    – When creating or editing a lot of chapter points, it is often helpful to arrange the windows to facilate the process. Figure 8-2 is a screen shot of how to arrange the windows for this task.

2. Once is open, notice the following feature of the timeline.

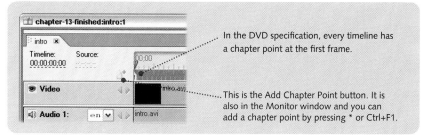

In the DVD specification, every timeline has a chapter point at the first frame.

This is the Add Chapter Point button. It is also in the Monitor window and you can add a chapter point by pressing * or Ctrl+F1.

– Because one chapter point is set automatically at the first frame of the timeline, you will have six chapters once all the chapter points are set.

3. Play the timeline once. Press the Space bar and the timeline will begin to play. When it finishes, press the Home key to jump back to the beginning of the timeline.

4. In the Timeline window, move the current time indicator (CTI), ▼, to 00;00;05;26. You can see the time update in two places: in the upper left-hand corner of the Timeline window and in the bottom center of the Monitor window. The frame shown onscreen should be a row of Victorian houses with downtown on the horizon.

5. With the CTI at this location, choose Timeline > Add Chapter Point. The second chapter point's marker, 📍, appears in the Timeline ruler.

6. Double-click the timeline's current time display, 00;00;06;20 . The blue text immediately changes to an editable field, 00;00;06;20 . Type 00;00;18;02 into the field and press Enter. The CTI moves to the new location. The frame shown onscreen should be the Transamerica building.

7. To set the third chapter point at this location, press Ctrl+F1.

8. This time you will set a chapter point on the fly and then zoom in to make precise adjustments. With either the Timeline or Monitor window in focus, press the Space bar. The timeline begins to play. Stop the timeline when you get close to 00;00;18;00.

9. This time, press the asterisk key, *, on the numeric keypad to set the fourth chapter point. If you set the chapter point a little before or after 18 seconds, do not worry, you will adjust the time next.

If you are using a laptop with no numeric keypad, press Ctrl+F1.

The Zoom In button is in the lower left corner of the Timeline window.

10. The next chapter actually starts at 00;00;18;04. To set it there, zoom into the timeline by pressing the Zoom In button, 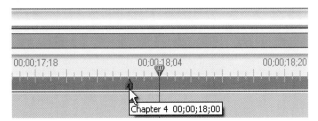, twice and then move the chapter point to this location by selecting it and dragging it to 00;00;18;04.

11. Now advance the timeline to 00;00;22;25. You should see a frame of the Haight-Ashbury street sign. To set the fifth chapter point, click the Add Chapter Point button, , in the Timeline window. It is located at the left side of the time ruler and is after the timeline (current) and Source clip time display.

12. For the last marker, move the CTI to 00;00;28;19. You should see a frame of a white truck passing and the beginning of a cable car coming onscreen. In the Monitor window, click on the Add Chapter Point button (it looks just like the one in the Timeline window mentioned in Step 11).

In Tutorial 19 on page 214, you will use these chapter points to create animated thumbnail buttons for a scene selection menu. Regular buttons, or buttons that are not video, can also link to chapters. When you select a button, you use the Properties palette and pick a chapter from the fly-out menu, or you can use the pickwhip to target a chapter point in a timeline or in the Timelines tab.

Setting Chapters on Untranscoded and Transcoded Assets

When Encore DVD transcodes AVI assets, the asset is converted into DVD-compliant MPEG-2 video. This variant of MPEG-2 follows strict formatting rules that break the video file into segments called GOPs, or groups of pictures. A GOP is a unit of 15 to 18 frames and the first frame of the unit is the GOP header.

Chapter points must be placed at GOP headers, which leaves two options when setting chapter points for DVD-Video. The first is to set the chapters in the AVI file before it is transcoded. When Encore DVD transcodes the file, it forces GOPs to begin at each chapter point, which preserves the location, except when chapter points are fewer than 18 frames apart for NTSC video and 15 frames apart for PAL video.

The second option is to set the chapters after transcoding. The drawback to this is that you cannot set a chapter on just any frame in the video—the chapter has to be on a GOP header frame. This might not be an issue if you set your chapter frames on a fade to black, but it can be tricky if you are placing chapters on transcoded video with jump cuts. In this case, the chapter points might not fall exactly where you want them.

I highly recommend setting chapters before you transcode your assets if chapter point placement is important to you. You can set chapters in Encore DVD or you can set them in Premiere Pro and export an MPEG-2 or AVI file. It will save the chapter points along with the video file.

Tutorial 15: Set the End Action and Menu Remote Button

The end action is the destination the DVD player shows when a timeline ends. Forgetting to set the end action causes the DVD player to go into Stop mode. The DVD does not return to a menu but shows a blank screen, which greatly disorients the viewer, so the end action should always be set.

The Menu Remote button should be the destination when the viewer presses the Menu button on a DVD remote control while the timeline is playing. In most cases, you can set the Menu Remote to be the same as the end action, but depending on the disc's flowchart, you might need to set it to something else.

In this tutorial, you will set the end action and then I will discuss a couple of ways to make sure it is set on a per project basis.

1. Open the Intro timeline if it is not open. Make sure nothing is selected inside the timeline, such as clips or chapter points.

2. Import *trolley-menu.psd*. It is located in the Chapter 15 folder.

3. Switch back to the TImeline window, examine the Properties palette, and look at the settings.

– The End Action property is the destination shown when the timeline ends. When this timeline ends, it needs to go to the Trolley menu.

Refer to "Using the Link Control" on page 159 and "Tutorial 7: Links" on page 194.

4. Setting an End Action property is exactly the same process as setting a button link, the first play, or the Remote Title property. Drag the pickwhip to the Trolley menu in the Project tab.

5. Setting the Menu Remote property is also the same as setting other links. Drag the pickwhip to the Trolley menu.

Subtitles

In most cases, subtitles are a timeline's dialog or narration shown as text in the lower third of the screen. The view accesses subtitles by chosing them on a menu or by pressing the Subtitle button on a DVD remote control. A collection of subtitles for any given language is placed on a single track in the timeline. A timeline can have up to 32 subtitles, and the viewer can display any one of the 32 subtitles at a time.

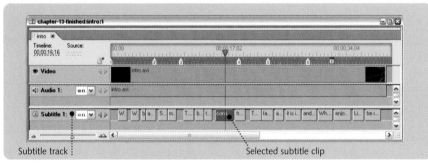

Subtitle track   Selected subtitle clip

Figure 8-2: **Subtitles in the timeline**

Like button subpictures, subtitles are 2-bit images comprising four colors. One color is the matte color, and the other three colors are used for the text fill, for the stroke, and to provide antialiasing between the fill and stroke colors (Figure 8-3).

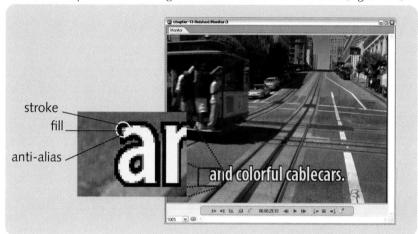

Figure 8-3: **Subtitle colors**

Adding subtitles is an optional step in the DVD authoring process and takes time to produce—especially for long sequences. My recommendation is to use a dedicated subtitle creation tool or hire a service to do the subtitle preparation in a form the Encore DVD supports. Encore DVD supports three subtitling formats.

- Captions Inc. (also referred to as Image Script format)
- FAB
- Text Script

Captions Inc. and FAB subtitle files are scripts that contain position information and links to image files that contain the subtitle text. Because the subtitle text is prerendered, neither of these formats can be edited.

Tutorial 16: Import Subtitles

In this tutorial, I show you how to import text format subtitles into the Intro timeline created in Tutorial 13.

1. Open the tutorial-13 project file you created at the end of Tutorial 13.
2. Open the Intro timeline.
3. Choose Timeline > Import Subtitles > Text Script....

– An Open dialog box appears. Navigate to the Tutorial 16 folder and open intro-subtitles.

4. The Import Subtitles dialog appears. It shows a preview from the position of the CTI in the timeline and presents formatting options, as well as the subtitle track on which the subtitles are placed.

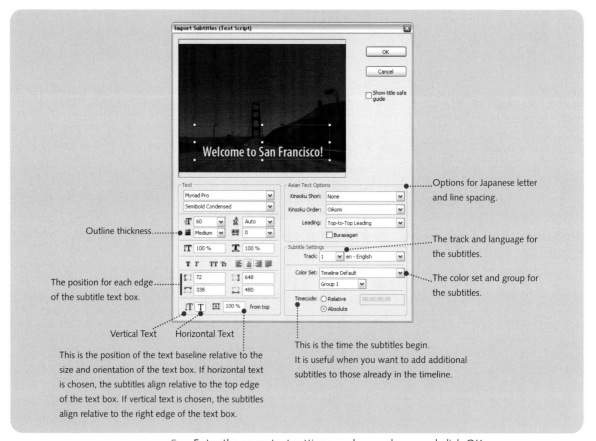

Outline thickness

The position for each edge of the subtitle text box

Vertical Text   Horizontal Text

This is the position of the text baseline relative to the size and orientation of the text box. If horizontal text is chosen, the subtitles align relative to the top edge of the text box. If vertical text is chosen, the subtitles align relative to the right edge of the text box.

Options for Japanese letter and line spacing.

The track and language for the subtitles.

The color set and group for the subtitles.

This is the time the subtitles begin. It is useful when you want to add additional subtitles to those already in the timeline.

5. Enter the same text settings as shown above and click OK.

– The subtitles are added to the timeline.

Creating Subtitles Externally and Internally

Creating Subtitles in Encore DVD

It is possible to create subtitles entirely in Encore DVD. The first step is to add a subtitle track to a timeline, move the CTI to where the subtitle begins, click inside the Monitor window with the Text tool, and begin typing. Using the timeline, you can trim individual subtitle clips or use the subtitle trimming tools in the Monitor window. However, you might find that it is faster to create subtitles externally.

Creating Subtitles Externally

Your options are to purchase a professional subtitling tool that creates a format that Encore DVD supports or to create subtitles manually. I have found limited success with enlarging the audio track header in Premiere Pro, previewing portions of audio, and entering the text in Notepad. The text format is detailed in Figure 8-4.

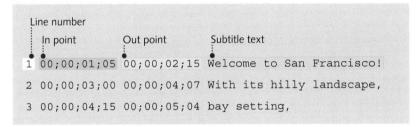

Figure 8-4: **Text subtitle format**

Each subtitle clip must begin with a line number. Following the line number are the subtitle clip's In and Out points. These time positions determine when the subtitle appears and disapears. The text after the out point is shown in the clip.

Subtitle Creation Tips

When creating subtitles, make each clip short enough to capture what is being said. When formatting subtitles, note that they are in the lower third of the screen. Do not choose large text because it will wrap to multiple lines and obscure the video.

Tutorial 17: Edit the Timeline Color Set

Timeline color sets are solely for subtitle fill, stroke, and antialias colors. A timeline color set is a lot like the color set for button highlights, but because subtitles are not interactive in a timeline, there is only one state (Figure 8-5).

	Fill/1	Stroke/2	Anti-alias/3
Subtitle Group 1	0%	0%	0%
Subtitle Group 2	100%	100%	100%
Subtitle Group 3	100%	100%	100%

Figure 8-5: **Timeline color sets**

Each timeline color set has three text color options available to a subtitle clip. These colors are used for the fill color and the stroke color and to provide partial antialiasing between the fill and stroke colors. Additionally, each color also has a transparency value ranging from 0 to 100 percent.

To determine the antialias color, add the fill and stroke red color values and divide by two. Repeat for the green and blue color values. Enter the resulting red, green, and blue colors for the antialias color.

 If two or three actors are onscreen, assign a different subtitle groups to each one to help the viewer determine which actor is speaking.

1. Open the Timeline window to the Intro timeline and open the Monitor window if it is not open.

2. Play the timeline or move the CTI until a subtitle clip is visible in the Monitor window.

3. Choose Edit > Color Sets > Timeline.

- The Timeline Color Set dialog appears.

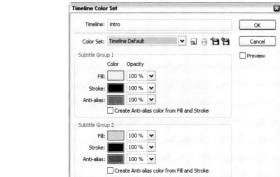

- Set the color options as you like them and select the checkbox for Preview.

- You can see the changes to the color set live in the Monitor window.

- Like the Menu Color Set dialog, you can copy, export, import, and delete color sets by pressing any of the buttons to the right of the color set drop-down menu.

4. If you like the changes you have made, click OK. If you do not want to save the changes you have made, click Cancel.

Tutorial 18: Set Links to Subtitles

Unlike the video and first audio track, additional audio or any subtitle text does not automatically appear unless you specify it in the Disc properties. Most DVDs provide a setup menu in which buttons link to a timeline and then instruct the player to show a subtitle track. In this tutorial, you will link the Play Subtitles button on the Trolley menu to the Intro timeline with the subtitles visible.

*For more information, refer to
"Disc Properties" on page 163.*

1. Open trolley-menu in the Project tab if it is not currently visible.

2. Select the Play Subtitles button and choose Object > Link to....

– The Specify Link dialog appears. This dialog shows every timeline and menu in the project.

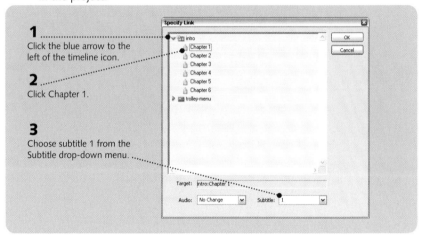

1
Click the blue arrow to the left of the timeline icon.

2
Click Chapter 1.

3
Choose subtitle 1 from the Subtitle drop-down menu.

3. Follow the steps in the illustration above and click OK.

4. Preview this new link by right-clicking anywhere on the Trolley menu and choosing Preview from Here. When the Preview window appears, click on the View Subtitles button to see the subtitles appear in the Intro timeline.

5. When finished previewing the subtitles, press the Escape (Esc) key to exit Preview mode.

Transcode Settings

For a discussion on how transcoding relates to motion menus, see page 20.

Most video and audio assets imported into a project need to be converted to MPEG-2 video before a DVD can be built. This process of converting raw assets to DVD-legal video and audio is called transcoding. Encore DVD uses the Edit Project Transcode Presets dialog to automatically transcode your assets based on internal bit budget calculations, or you can specify how assets are transcoded by selecting or creating a transcoding preset.

VIEWING TRANSCODE STATUS IN THE PROJECT TAB

The transcode settings column is in the Project tab. For video and audio assets, it lists Automatic, a preset name, Transcoded, or Don't Transcode. The Automatic setting means Encore DVD will calculate the optimum bitrate at build time. If a preset name is in the column, you have chosen a transcoding preset for the asset. When Transcoded appears in the Transcode Status column, an MPEG-2 audio or video stream or both has been created from the asset. This occurs after the project has been built or if the asset has been explicitly transcoded.

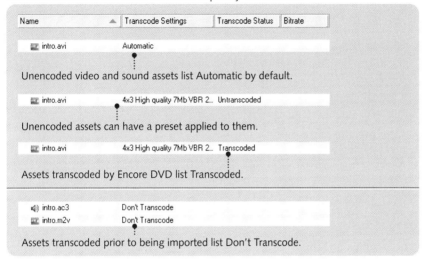

Figure 8-6: **Transcode settings**

If you have imported assets that are already DVD-legal MPEG-2 or AC3 files, these assets will show Don't Transcode in the Transcode Status column.

Using a Preset

Encore DVD ships with several transcode presets for both NTSC and PAL projects. A preset can be applied to an asset one of three ways.

1. Select the asset and choose a preset from the File > Transcode > Transcode Settings menu.

2. Right-click the asset in the Project tab and choose a preset from the context menu's Transcode Settings submenu.

3. Select the asset and choose a preset from the asset's Properties palette.

TRANSCODING AN ASSET ON DEMAND

If you want to transcode an asset before the DVD is built, select the asset in the Project tab and choose File > Transcode > Transcode Now. This will transcode the asset automatically or by the chosen preset.

Transcoding a DVD-legal asset is not recommended, but if the asset has a high bitrate that blows the bit budget, then go ahead.

The Transcode Now menu option is disabled for imported assets that are DVD-legal. In order to transcode a DVD-legal asset, you select a preset or choose the Automatic setting for this asset, enabling the Transcode Now option.

TRANSCODING AN ASSET AGAIN

If you are not satisfied with the transcoding process, you can choose another preset using the first two options. If you need to see how the original asset looked before transcoding, you can choose File > Transcode > Revert to Original.

Creating Custom Presets

Although in Encore DVD, the dialog is called Project Transcode Presets.

In most cases, the Automatic setting or one of Encore DVD's preinstalled transcode presets will suffice. In cases in which they do not, or if you want to see what the available settings are, you can choose File > Transcode > Edit Project Transcode Presets.... This shows the Adobe Media Encoder. This is the same Encoder interface that is shown in Premiere Pro and After Effects. The difference is that Encore DVD only shows and creates presets that are DVD-legal. The presets in Encore DVD can only create MPEG-2 and PCM or Dolby Digital audio; they cannot create video for Windows Media, QuickTime, or Real Media. The presets are based on the chosen television standard. An NTSC project only shows NTSC presets and a PAL project only shows PAL presets.

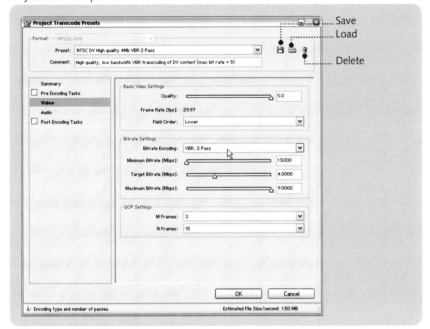

..... Save
..... Load

..... Delete

Figure8-9:The Project Transcode Presets dialog

1. Choose File > Transcode > Edit Project Transcoding Presets...(Figure 8-9).

2. Select a preset from the Preset drop-down list.

3. By default, a summary for the preset appears in the control area. It is organized by video and audio properties.

4. When finished inspecting the properties, click OK.

To create a preset do the following.

1. Choose File > Transcode > Edit Project Transcoding Presets...

2. Select a preset from the Presets drop-down list to use as the basis for the new preset.

3. Summarize the new preset in the Comment field.

4. Adjust the new preset's audio and video properties as needed.

5. When finished, click the Save button.

6. Enter a name for the preset in the Save Preset dialog and click OK.

7. Click OK in the Project Transcode Presets dialog.

 Presets are part of the Project; they are not part of the Encore DVD application preferences.

Motion Menus

For more information on properties pertaining to motion menus, see "Motion Menus" on page 32.

Many DVD viewers find motion menus more appealing because they appreciate the production effort that goes into creating the animation. A well-crafted motion menu can lure people to a kiosk or make someone laugh before they watch a video segment. The end of this chapter covers creating simple motion menus—ones that can be easily created in Encore DVD without having to do the animation in After Effects. If you are looking for information on how to create looping menus and menus with transitions, wait until the next chapter.

Tutorial 19: Create Animated Thumbnails

DVDs created for Hollywood films include a scene selection menu. These menus often have buttons that are a representative image from scenes in the movie. This menu is a convenient way to return to a scene in the film without having to fast forward from the beginning. In some scene selection menus, the buttons are animated and show a brief selection of video from the scene. This type of button is called an animated thumbnail button and is easy to create in Encore DVD.

This is great benefit of DVDs over VHS!

Before Encore DVD, a scene selection menu would have required the use of Adobe After Effects to composite frames from each scene onto a background image. With Encore DVD, this is a fairly simple task.

Set chapter points (and poster frames if neccessary) in the timeline.

*   Create buttons that contain a layer with a (%) prefix, which instructs Encore DVD to place video inside the shape of the layer.

*   Link the buttons to the chapter points.

In this tutorial, you will link the chapter points in the Intro timeline to the Trolley menu and create a poster frame for Chapter 6.

1. Open the Trolley menu.

2. Select each of the six thumbnail buttons and link them to the six chapters in the Intro timeline. Link Chapter 1 to the button in the top left-hand corner, and link Chapter 2 to the button to the immediate right.

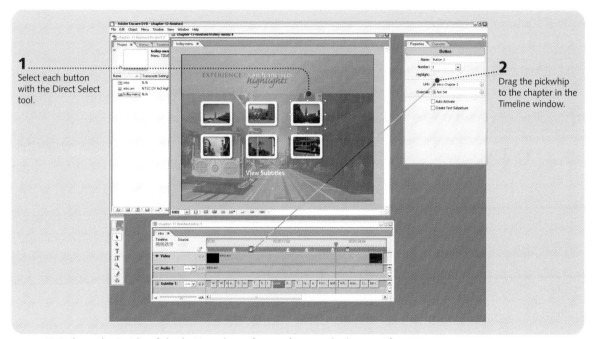

1
Select each button with the Direct Select tool.

2
Drag the pickwhip to the chapter in the Timeline window.

–   Note how the inside of the buttons have frames from each chapter. If you open the Layers palette and look inside the button layer set for each of these buttons, you will see that the (%) layer is where the video frames are placed.

3. Now look at Chapter 6. It should represent the wonderful cable cars of San Francisco, but unfortunately, the footage begins with an ugly white truck passing in front of the camera.

BEFORE   **AFTER**

– Chapter points have an additional property that solves this very problem—a poster frame. A poster frame is a substitute frame to use for the chapter in thumbnail buttons. Use the Poster Frame property for this case and the case in which you want to the chapter to begin at a fade up from black but you want the button to show a more representative frame from the chapter.

4. To select a poster frame for Chapter 6, select it in the Timeline window, move the CTI to 00;00;32;02, and choose Timeline > Set Poster Frame. Now that the buttons all have good frames, you can add the motion.

5. Switch to the Menu Editor window and choose Edit > Deselect All so the menu's properties are visible in the Properties palette.

6. Note that the menu is set to Hold Forever. This is one mean property when it is enabled because while it is on, the menu will not animate. Think of it as a spell cast on the menu.

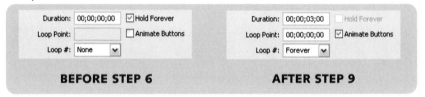

BEFORE STEP 6   **AFTER STEP 9**

– Begin by unchecking the Hold Forever checkbox.

7. Now check the Animate Buttons checkbox. This property will instruct Encore DVD to pull video from each chapter and place it inside the (%) thumbnail layers.

8. Set a duration for the menu. Besides being the menu's duration in time, it is also the number of video frames to pull for each chapter button. Enter a duration of 3 seconds (00;00;03;00) in the Duration field.

9. Select Forever in the Loop # drop-down list. This will cause the menu to loop forever until the viewer selects one of the buttons.

10. To preview this menu with the motion, choose File > Render Motion Menus.

– When the Render Motion menus progress dialog appears, check Preview when complete.

Tutorial 20: Create a Menu with Audio

It might sound a little odd, but a motion menu can be a still menu with audio playing in the background. Most people think motion menus require video, but the combination of audio and a still graphic is also a legitimate motion menu. Given this, a motion menu should really be thought of as a menu that includes time-based media such as audio or video or both. In this tutorial, you will add a short audio clip to a still menu.

1. Open the tutorial-20 Encore DVD project file. It is located in the Tutorial 20 folder.

2. The purpose of this tutorial is soley to demonstrate how audio and a still menu can create a motion menu, so the project has only a single menu.

3. Import the sound file that will be added to the menu. Choose File > Import and select the named audio file loop in the Tutorial 20 folder.

4. Now open the Points menu and show the Properties palette (press F5).

   – Below the End Action and Override link controls are two additional properties for Video and Audio. For this tutorial, you are only interested in the Audio link control.

5. Drag the pickwhip for the Audio property to the loop audio asset in the Project tab.

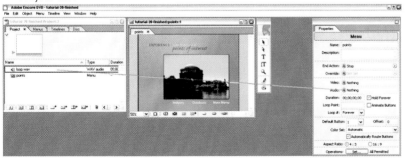

6.   Now you need to set the additional menu properties so that this menu will loop indefinitely and play the audio. Set the Loop property to Forever.

Building Projects

In DVD terms, compiling a project is called multiplexing or "muxing."

Building a project takes all the menus, subpictures, timelines, subtitles, navigation, and color sets and compiles it all into a DVD-Video–formatted disc, folder, DVD disc image file, or DLT (digital linear tape) archive.

Building a DVD Disc

To build a DVD disc, choose File > Build Project > Build DVD Disc. You can write the current project, a volume, or a DVD disc image file to a disc. This option muxes your project to recordable media such as a CD-R, CD-RW, DVD-R, DVD-RW, DVD+R, or DVD+RW.

 To see Encore DVD's listing of supported drives go to http://www.adobe.com/products/encore/systemreqs.html.

Burning a project to a CD restricts the size of your project to the size of the CD recordable media. Although DVD content burned to CD recordable media is playable on a computer, it is not generally supported by DVD set-top players.

To build a DVD disc do the following.

1.   Insert the blank disc into the recordable drive.

2.   Choose File > Build DVD > Make DVD Disc.

  – If you are prompted to save the project, save it. If you want to create a variation of the project, click Cancel and save the project as new version before choosing Make DVD Disc again.

For more information on the Check Links dialog, see "Checking Links" on page 130.

  – If broken links are found in your project, you are asked whether to correct them or ignore them. It is recommended that you fix all broken links.

3.   In the Make DVD Disc dialog, select the drive containing the blank disc and click Next.

  – If you have more than one recordable drive attached, select the one you want to use from the Recorder drop-down list.

  – If the drive does not appear, click Search to refresh the Recorder list.

4.   Click Build in the Summary window.

Building a DVD Image or Folder

to build either a readable DVD folder or DVD disc image on the hard disk, choose File > Build Project > Build DVD Image or Build DVD Folder.

Use a software DVD player that mounts a folder or disc image. This saves DVD recordable media and money.

Building a DVD Master to DLT

Building a DVD Master assumes you have a digital linear tape (DLT) drive attached to your computer. It also assumes that you are ready to send your project on DLT to a replicator, a facility where glass masters are created from the DLT and are used to create hundreds or thousands of copies.

To build a DVD master, choose File > Build Project > Build DVD Master. You can write the current project, a volume, or a DVD disc image to DLT.

PROJECT SETTINGS PERTAINING TO THE CREATION OF A DLT

When creating a DLT for replication, a host of Project options becomes available to you. These additional settings are accessible by clicking Project Settings in the Disc tab. Note that these options are only functional when mastering to DLT; they do not work for recordable media such as DVD+R or DVD-R.

For more information on project settings, see "Accessing Additional Project Settings" on page 145.

Additional Techniques

In this last chapter I discuss 16:9 menus, slideshows, and advanced motion menu techniques.

Creating 16:9 Menus

A 16:9 has an aspect ratio similiar to that of film. The main reason to create menus with a 16:9 aspect ratio is to watch video that was shot with a camera that produces 16:9 images.

For more information on 16:9 and 4:3 aspect ratios, refer to "Frame Aspect Ratio" on page 27.

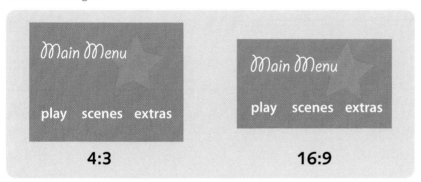

Figure 9-1: **4:3 and 16:9 aspect ratios**

Insert the book's DVD into your computer and open the Tutorials folder. Copy the Chapter 9 folder to the local hard disk before beginning these tutorials.

Tutorial 21: Create a 16:9 Still Menu in Photoshop
In this tutorial, you will crop and resize a digital photo to a 16:9 NTSC DVD resolution and use it as the background for a menu.

For more information on non-square pixels, see "Pixel Aspect Ratio" on page 28.

STEPS IN PHOTOSHOP
1.   Launch Photoshop and choose File > Open.

   – Navigate to the Tutorial 21 folder, select homes, and click Open.

– As mentioned earlier, the photograph is a four-megapixel image with roughly a 4:3 aspect ratio. You need to crop and resize it.

Choose Window > Options if the Options bar is not currently visible.

2. Select the Marquee tool, ⬚. In the Options bar, choose Fixed Aspect Ratio for the style, and enter 16 for the width and 9 for the height. Also make sure the feather is set to 0.

3. With the Marquee tool, drag a selection over the image.

4. Choose Image > Crop. The image is cropped to the proper aspect ratio, but now you need to size it for DVD. Follow Step 5 if you are using Photoshop CS or Step 6 if you are using Photoshop 7.

5. If you are using Photoshop CS, resize the image to 720 pixels wide by 480 pixels tall and then choose a pixel aspect ratio of 1.2. Because Photoshop CS supports nonsquare pixel aspect ratios, you can properly prepare images for video display.

    –   Choose Image > Image Size. In the Image Size dialog, turn off Constrain Proportions, and turn on Resample Image. Even though this will distort the image, you will correct the distortion by adjusting the image's pixel aspect ratio.

    –   Enter 720 for the width and 480 for the height and click OK.

    –   Choose Image > Pixel Aspect Ratio > D1/DV NTSC Widescreen (1.2). Notice how the image appears correct.

    –   Continue to Step 7.

6. If you are using Photoshop 7, resize the image to 864 pixels wide by 480 pixels high. Because earlier versions of Photoshop did not support nonsquare pixel aspect ratios, you need to allow for more horizontal resolution.

    – Choose Image > Image Size. In the Image Size dialog, turn on Constrain Proportions, and turn on Resample Image.

    – Enter 864 for the width and 480 for the height and click OK.

    – Continue to Step 7.

7.   Choose File > Save and choose Photoshop file format if it is not already choosen. Save the file in the Tutorial 21 folder.

8.   Open the file *alamo-square.psd* in the Tutorial 21 folder. It has a background image and text layer that you'll use for this menu. Drag both the layers for the alamo-square image and text from the menu into the main-16:9 document.

9.   Create a background for the buttons. Select the Rectangle shape tool, ▢ , and draw a shape over the bottom third of the document.

10.   Open the file *buttons.psd* It has buttons that can be copied into this menu. Link the layer sets by pressing the link layer well, 🔗 , for each layer.

STARTING A WIDESCREEN MENU FROM SCRATCH

In Photoshop, to create a new 16:9 menu from scratch, pick one of the widescreen presets in the New File dialog, which is accessed by choosing File > New. If you are using Photoshop CS, select the NTSC DV Widescreen 720 x 480 (with guides) preset. If you are using Photoshop 7, select the 864 x 480 wide NTSC DV/DVD preset.

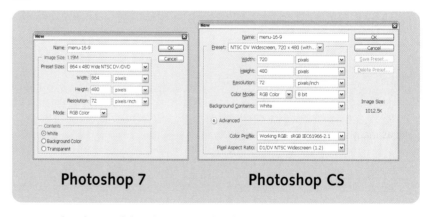

Figure 9-2: **Photoshop 7 and Photoshop CS New File dialogs**

 Photoshop CS supports nonsquare pixels. Earlier versions do not, which is why the Photoshop 7 preset has more horizontal pixels.

CREATE A 16:9 MENU IN ENCORE DVD

Encore DVD has a blank template for 16:9 menus in the Library palette. Select it and click the New Menu button, ⊞⁺, at the bottom of the Library palette. From there, use the Text tool to create headlines and button text, and import images and video to use as design elements and backgrounds.

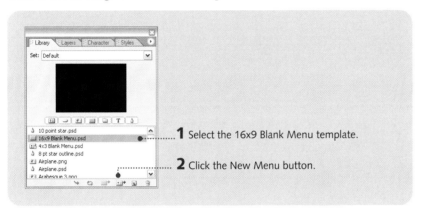

1 Select the 16x9 Blank Menu template.

2 Click the New Menu button.

Figure 9-3: **Library palette**

Creating Slideshows

The DVD is an excellent medium for presenting photographic slideshows given the large capacity of DVD-Video discs and the growing prevalence of DVD players. The two methods for presenting a slideshow on the DVD are in a timeline or as a series of linked menus.

Tutorial 22: Create a Slideshow in a Timeline

TImeline-based slideshows are easier to create in Encore DVD than menu-based slideshows because they are created in fewer steps and they do not require you to set as many links.

1. Create a new project by choosing File > New.

2. Choose File > Import. In the Tutorial 22 folder, drag a selection around all the images and click Open.

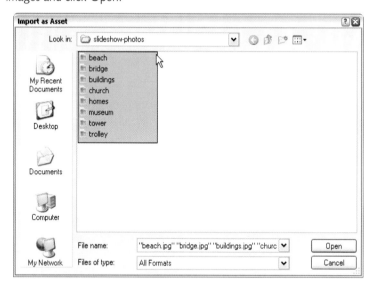

3. Once the images have been added to the project, create a new timeline. Press Ctrl+T. Zoom out in time by adjusting the time zoom slider in the timeline window. Move it a few notches to the left.

4. In the Project tab, drag a marquee around the images you just imported and drag them to the new timeline.

    – The slideshow wizard appears. In the dialog, enter a time of 6 seconds and click OK. All of these images now appear as still image clips in the Timeline window's video track.

If the slideshow wizard does not appear, it is because the preference to show it has been turned off. Choose Edit > Timeline > Preferences and turn on Show Still Wizard.

5. In order for these images to appear correctly in the slideshow, you will set the Scale in Still Clip properties dialog to Scale and Apply Matte.

- This option scales the clips proportionally to a 4:3 aspect ratio in the project's television standard (NTSC in this case) and applies black to either the top and bottom of the screen or to the left or right depending on the aspect ratio of the photo. If the photo has a 4:3 aspect ratio, no scaling is applied.

- Notice the Monitor window. Choose Window > Monitor if it is not open. Press the Home key and then click the Play button, ▶, to preview the slideshow.

- Notice how each still clip is 6 seconds in duration—the default length in time for stills.

- In the Timeline window, notice that a chapter point is placed automatically at the start of each still.

6. Choose File > Save and save the project in the Tutorial 22 folder. Name the project "tutorial-22" and click Save.

 If a shorter or longer default length is desired, choose Edit > Preferences > Timeline and specify a different time in the Default Still Length text field.

Tutorial 23: Create a Slideshow with Menus

Presenting a slideshow as a series of menus has a few advantages over slideshows that are presented in timelines. Menus, if they are set to Hold Forever, are in a paused state by default, which allows the user to advance forward and backward through a set of photos.

1. Launch Encore DVD and open the Tutorial-23 project.

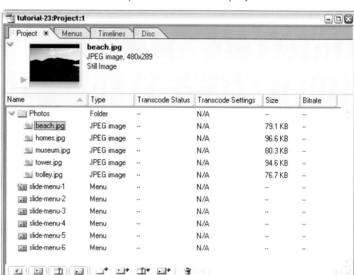

- Look at the Project tab. It has one menu and a folder with five photographs. You will copy and create duplicates of this menu, rename and number the duplicates, replace the images in each, and create links between them.

2. Select slide-menu-1 in the Project tab and choose Edit > Copy or press Ctrl+C. The menu is now copied to the clipboard. Choose Edit > Paste or press Ctrl+V. A duplicate of the menu appears in the Project tab. Rename it "slide-menu-2" by right-clicking on it and choosing Rename from the contextual menu.

- Repeat Step 2 four more times to create slide-menu-3, -4, -5 and -6.

3. Click-drag a selection marquee around the six menus in the Project tab and press the Enter key to open all menus simultaneously into one Menu Editor window.

4. Now you need to replace the photo of the Palace of Fine Arts with the other San Francisco photos.

- Click on the tab for slide-menu-2 in the Menu Editor window.

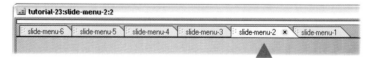

- Move over to the Project tab and open the Photos folder if it is not open already. Select the beach photo and drag it to the Menu Editor window. Place it so it occupies the same place as the Palace photo.

- Choose Window > Layers, select the Palace layer, and press Delete.

- Repeat these steps to place the remaining photos in the remaining menus.

5. In this step, you are going to use the Menus tab and the Properties palette to set all the links between these menus. Although you cannot see the menus and the buttons, all have similiar names. You can use a few Menus tab tricks to sort the list and create all these links quickly.

- Choose Window > Menus

- Drag-select a marquee around all the menus in the Menus tab. In the Buttons pane below, all the buttons in all of those menus will appear simultaneously.

- Now you need to set the correct headings in the Buttons pane. The headings should look like those in Figure 9-4, with the Menu column heading as the sort column.

- Select the Next button for slide-menu-1 and use the pickwhip, ⊚, to drag it to the slide-menu-2 menu in the pane above. Select this menu's Previous button and link it to slide-menu-6. When you are finished, the window should look like this:

For more information on configuring the column headings, see Sorting and Filtering the View on page 128.

Name	Menu ▲	Link
Next	slide-menu-1	slide-menu-2:Default
Previous	slide-menu-1	slide-menu-6:Default
Next	slide-menu-2	slide-menu-3:Default
Previous	slide-menu-2	slide-menu-1:Default
Next	slide-menu-3	slide-menu-4:Default
Previous	slide-menu-3	slide-menu-5:Default
Next	slide-menu-4	slide-menu-5:Default
Previous	slide-menu-4	slide-menu-3:Default
Next	slide-menu-5	slide-menu-6:Default
Previous	slide-menu-5	slide-menu-4:Default
Next	slide-menu-6	slide-menu-1:Default
Previous	slide-menu-6	slide-menu-5:Default

6. Preview the project and test the links.

Advanced Motion Menu Techniques

On many of the online forums dedicated to Encore DVD, the number one request is how to create motion menus with transitions. In the next two tutorials, I present a fully animated composition and discuss which properties in the After Effects Render Queue window facilitate motion menu production.

Tutorial 24: Create a Looping Motion Menu

The composition has an animated headline that falls from above and bounces and a subordinate headline and buttons that fade in afterwards. Following this introductory animation, the camera switches focus between the headline and subordinate headline.

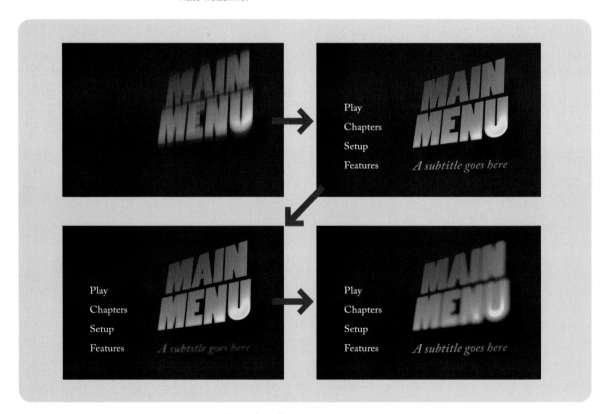

Figure 9-4: **Frames from the motion menu**

In this tutorial, the same composition is exported twice. The first export creates a video file containing only the frame from where the menu loops, known as the loop point. The second export contains the entire animation. Exporting the loop frame assists in aligning subpicture highlights with the buttons that are rendered into the movie.

STEPS IN AFTER EFFECTS

1. Open the After Effects file "looping-menu" in the Tutorial 24 folder.

    If you have not copied the tutorial folder to your local hard drive, do so now.

2. In the Project window, double-click the main-menu-bg composition.

    –   Notice the Loop Point layer marker at 4 seconds on the Camera 1 layer. This is where the loop begins for the menu.

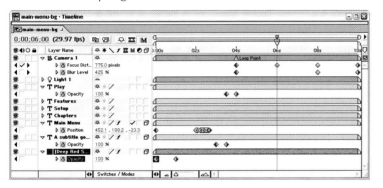

3. Choose Composition > Add to Render Queue.

    –   The main-menu-bg composition is added to the render queue.

4. Open the Render Queue window by choosing Window > Render Queue.

    –   Click on the hot text or "hot text for Render Settings. In the Time Sampling group box, click Set. In the Custom Time Span dialog, enter 0;00;04;00 for

    If you would like to preview the menu animation, press The 0 key on the numerical keypad or choose Composition > Preview > Ram Preview.

both the Start and End frames and click OK. Click OK in the Render Settings dialog.

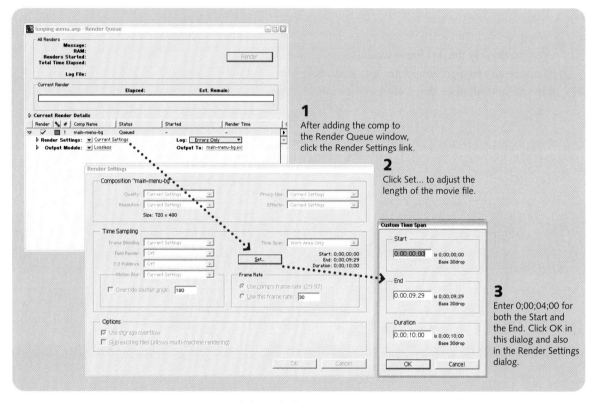

1

After adding the comp to the Render Queue window, click the Render Settings link.

2

Click Set... to adjust the length of the movie file.

3

Enter 0;00;04;00 for both the Start and the End. Click OK in this dialog and also in the Render Settings dialog.

– Now click on the hot text main-menu-bg.avi. In the Output Movie dialog, save the single-frame AVI file as *main-menu-bg-loop-frame.avi* and click Save.

5. Click back into the Timeline or Composition window for main-menu-bg, and choose Composition > Add to Render Queue again.

    – A second entry is created for main-menu-bg in the render queue.

6. Open the render queue window again and save it to the same location as the first frame version of the animation. The animation will render completely.

7. With both versions added to the render queue, click Render. Once the renders are complete, quit After Effects and continue to the next section.

INITIAL STEPS IN ENCORE DVD

Now you need to create a project and import the movie files. In these initial steps, you will use the single-frame movie to create a motion menu . This is important to do, because the single-frame movie shows all the buttons. Encore DVD does not offer playback of motion menus in the Menu Editor, so if you were to use the fully rendered movie, only the first frame would show in the Menu Editor and you would not be able to align subpictures with buttons. In the final steps, you will swap the full animation for the single frame and set the remaining motion menu properties.

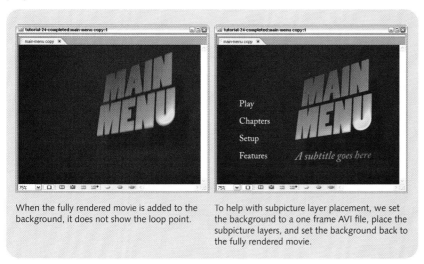

When the fully rendered movie is added to the background, it does not show the loop point.

To help with subpicture layer placement, we set the background to a one frame AVI file, place the subpicture layers, and set the background back to the fully rendered movie.

Figure 9-5: **The first frames for the two movies**

1. Launch Encore DVD.

2. Import the two files. Choose File > Import....

    – Navigate to the Tutorial 24 folder, select both movie files, and click Open.

3. Choose File > Save. Save the project file in the Tutorials 24 folder and name it tutorial-24.

4. Create a new menu with *4x3Blank Menu.psd* in the Library palette. Select the menu and press the New Menu button, ⊞✦, at the bottom of the Library palette.

    – Select the menu in the Project tab and choose Edit > Rename or press Shift+Ctrl+R. Rename the menu "main-menu" and click OK.

5.   In the menu's Properties palette, set the menu background to the *main-menu-bg-loop-frame.avi* file. Drag the pickwhip, 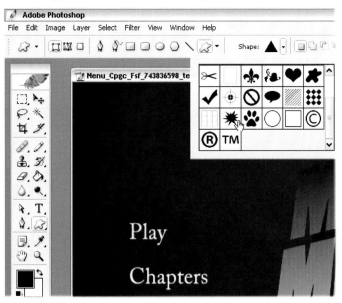, to the file in the Project tab. The background is replaced with the menu's loop point.

6.   Choose File > Save.

7.   Press the Edit in Photoshop button, , in the toolbar. Once the menu opens in Photoshop, continue to the next section.

STEPS IN PHOTOSHOP

You need to create buttons for the menu in Photoshop, but you do not need to create the text for the buttons because they were already rendered into the video backgrounds created in After Effects. What you do need to create, however, are subpicture layers, as well as hotspots for use on software-based DVD players.

1.   Select the Custom Shape tool, , in the Tool palette.

2.   In the Options bar, select a shape to use for the custom shape. I like to use the Startbust shape, but free to use another if you like.

–   Create a shape to the left of the word Play. Double-click on the shape's color swatch in the Layers palette and pick an orange color that will work with the red and yellow present in the menu.

– In the Layers palette, rename the layer to (=1).

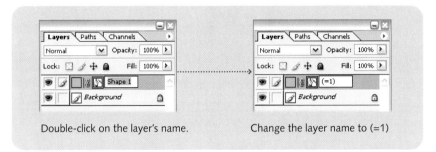

Double-click on the layer's name.   Change the layer name to (=1)

3. Now you need to add another invisible layer because currently, the button's hotspot will be calculated only from the startburst. You need to increase the clickable area so that viewers will be able to click on Play and activate the button when they use a software DVD player.

4. To create this invisible hotspot, select the Rectangular shape tool, ▢ , and draw a shape layer that covers the word Play entirely. In the Layer palette, click on the layer, set its opacity to 0 percent, and click its eye , ● , to turn visibility off.

– Even though visibility is off, when this layer is added to a button layer set, Encore DVD will use the layer's nonvisible bounds to create the button hotspot, or clickable area. This technique is analogous to creating image maps in HTML authoring tools such as GoLive.

5. Now link the subpicture layer and the invisible hotspot layer and choose Layer > New > Layer Set from Linked….

– In the New Set from Linked dialog, use the Encore DVD layer naming convention and name the set (+) Play.

6. Repeat Steps 1 through 5 for the remaining buttons. When finished, choose File > Save and quit Photoshop.

FINAL STEPS IN ENCORE DVD

The menu should now have button layer sets for all four buttons. Open the Layers palette in Encore DVD and turn on one of the subpicture preview states by clicking one of the buttons at the bottom of the Menu Editor, or choose View > Show Activated Subpicture.

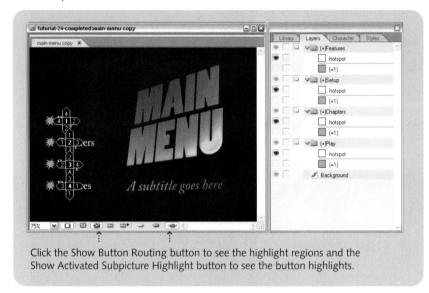

Click the Show Button Routing button to see the highlight regions and the Show Activated Subpicture Highlight button to see the button highlights.

Figure 9-6: **Main menu with subpictures and highlights created in Photoshop**

1. Open the Properties palette for main-menu and set the video background to the fully animated movie, *main-menu-bg.avi*. Use the pickwhip, ⊚, or press the Alt key while dragging the video asset from the Project tab to the Menu Editor window.

See Table 6-26 on page 150 for more information on the Loop Point property.

2. In the Properties palette, set Loop Point to 00;00;04;00 and set the Loop # property to Forever. Save the project. With the loop point set 4 seconds into the animation, the menu will play completely from start to finish the first time; when the animation ends, the menu will return to the loop point.

3. Preview the project by clicking the Project Preview button in the Tool palette or by choosing File > Project Preview.

Tutorial 25: Create an Exit Transition

Assume the client liked the introductory animation and now wants to see the menu fade to black before going to one of the link destinations. This is accomplished by rendering a movie in which the menu fades to black, placing the movie in a menu, setting all of the buttons on the main-menu to link to the transitional menu, and finally setting the Override property for each button to go to the appropriate link.

STEPS WITH AFTER EFFECTS

1. Open the After Effects project file named *transition-animation.aep*. It is located in the Tutorial 25 folder.

   If you have not copied the tutorial folder to your local hard drive, do so now.

2. Open the main-menu-bg composition and move the CTI to 0;00;04;00.

3. Choose Composition > Save Frame As > File or press Ctrl+Alt+S. Save the file to the Tutorial 25 folder.

   – After Effects does not immediately create the file but adds it as a task to the render queue.

   – You do not need a layered Photoshop file because all you need to do is fade a composite frame of the menu to black.

4. Open the Render Queue window and expand the Output Module category.

   – Select Import from the Post-Render Action drop-down menu.

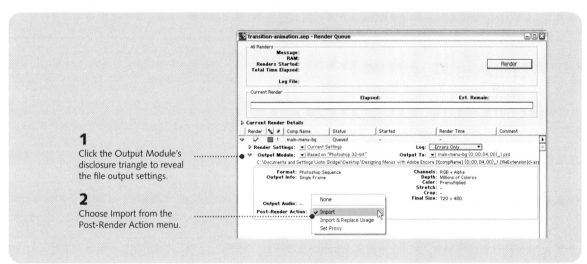

1

Click the Output Module's disclosure triangle to reveal the file output settings.

2

Choose Import from the Post-Render Action menu.

   – This will import the file into the project after it is rendered.

5. Click the Render button.

6. In the Project window, click-drag the newly created file, *main-menu-bg (0;00;04;00).psd*, to the New Composition button, ⊡ , at the bottom of the Project window.

– You will now see a composition that has the file as the only layer. Now you need to adjust the duration of the composition and then set some opacity keyframes.

7. Choose Compostion > Composition Settings... or press Ctrl+K.

– Change the name of the composition to main-menu-transition.

– Change the duration to 0;00;06;00.

– Click OK.

8. Choose Composition > Background Color... or press Ctrl+Shift+B.

– If the color swatch is not already black, set it to black by clicking the eye dropper and sampling black from somewhere on the screen.

– Click OK.

9. Now select the *main-menu-bg (0;00;04;00).psd* layer in the Timeline window.

– Press T on the keyboard, to show the opacity. Click the stopwatch, ⏱, next to the opacity value. This sets an opacity keyframe of 100%, or full opacity.

10. Now press the End key on the keyboard or move the CTI to 00;00;06;00.

– Click the opacity value and enter 0. The screen will now turn black because the menu layer is fully transparent.

11. Choose Composition > Add to Render Queue. Save the file to the Tutorial 25 folder.

12. Click on the Render button and once the render is complete, quit After Effects and continue to the next section.

STEPS WITHIN ENCORE DVD

1. Launch Encore DVD and open the tutorial-25 project file.

2. Import the *main-menu-transition-avi* movie file, create a blank 4:3 menu, and add the movie file to the background.

3. In the Properties palette, set the menu's end action to return to main-menu. Keep the Loop # property set to None.

4. Open main-menu, link the Chapter button to the main-menu-transition menu, and set the Override property for the chapter button to Chapter-menu.

5. Preview the project by clicking the Preview button, 🔘, in the Tool palette.

You do not need to worry about where the end action goes because the buttons from the main-menu are going to override this link every time. It's good practice to set it to the previous menu in case one of the previous menu's buttons is not set.

Bibliography

Interface Design and Usability

Mullet, Kevin and Sano, Darell. 1995. *Designing Visual Interfaces.* Prentice Hall, Englewood Cliffs, NJ. ISBN 0-13-303389-9.

Nielsen, Jakob. 1993. *Usability Engineering.* Academic Press, Inc., Chestnut Hill, MA. ISBN 0-12-518406-9.

Graphic Design

Meggs, Phillip. 1983. *A History of Graphic Design*. Van Nostrand Reinhold, New York, NY. ISBN 0-442-31895-2.

Muller-Brockman, Josef. 1981. *Grid Systems in Graphic Design*. Verlag Niggli AG, Sulgen, Switzerland. ISBN 3-7212-0145-0.

Ruder, Emil. 1967. *Typography.* Verlag Niggli AG, Sulgen, Switzerland. ISBN 3-7212-0043-8.

Tracy, Walter. 1986. *Letters of Credit*. David Goodine, Publisher Inc., Boston, MA. ISBN 0-87923-636-1.

Animation and Filmmaking

Johnston, Ollie and Thomas, Frank. 1981. *The Illusion of Life: Disney Animation*. New York, New York. ISBN 0-7868-6070-7.

Katz, Steven D. 1991. *Film Directing Shot by Shot*. Michael Wiese Productions, Studio City, CA. ISBN 0-941188-10-8.

——. 1992. *Film Directing Cinematic Motion*. Michael Wiese Productions, Studio City, CA. ISBN 0-941188-10-8.

DVD Authoring and Digital Video

LaBarge, Ralph. 2001. *DVD Authoring and Production*. CMP Books, Lawrence, KS. ISBN 1-57820-082-2.

Taylor, Jim. 1998. *DVD Demystified*. McGraw-Hill, New York, NY. ISBN 0-07-135026-8.

Index

TV monitors, 40, 98, 100–101, 141. *See also* computer monitors

typefaces. *See also* text
choosing, 91–92
classifications, 69–76
display, 75–76, 93
families, 77–83, 156
formats, 89–90
included with Encore DVD, 92–93
for logos, 191–192
measurements, 85–89, 156
parts of, 66–69
in Photoshop, 175
punctuation marks, 83–85
styles, 77–83, 156
symbol, 84–85, 93

typography, 66–93

U

Unicode, 84
usability testing, 35–36, 57–64
user interface, Encore DVD, 123–167
user operations, 24–28, 133, 152, 154–155, 184
user research, 35–43
users, 39–41, 60–61. *See also* audiences; usability testing

V

vector artwork, 191–192
velocity graph, 112
VHS tapes, 45–46
video, 19–22, 162
video assets, 125
video camera, 8, 120–121
video cards, 7
video clips, trimming, 162
video decks, 8
video files, importing, 198–200
video footage, 24, 45
video-safe margins, 95–96
video streams, 20
video title sets (VTS), 197
viewers. *See* audiences; users
Visio program, 5

VOB (Video Object) files, 125
VTS (video title sets), 197

W

WAV format, 125
web site, companion to book, 3
whiteboards, 47–48
wireframes, 51–54
workflows, 169
workspaces, 165

X

x coordinates, 11–12
x-height, 68–69

Y

y coordinates, 11–12

Z

zoom controls, 120–121, 141, 166, 202

Creating Motion Graphics with After Effects

Volume 1: The Essentials, 3rd Edtion

Trish Meyer & Chris Meyer

Master the core concepts and tools you need to tackle virtually every job, including keyframe animation, masking, mattes, and plug-in effects. New chapters demystify Parenting, 3D Space, and features of the latest software version.

$59.95, 4-color, Trade Paper with CD-ROM, 448 pp, ISBN 1-57820-249-3

Photoshop CS for Nonlinear Editors

2nd Edtion

Richard Harrington

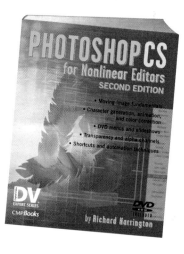

Use Photoshop CS to generate characters, correct colors, and animate graphics for digital video. You'll grasp the fundamental concepts and master the complete range of Photoshop tools through lively discourse, full-color presentations, and hands-on tutorials. The companion DVD contains 90 minutes of video lessons, tutorial media, and plug-ins.

$54.95, 4-color, Trade Paper with DVD, 336 pp, ISBN 1-57820-237-X

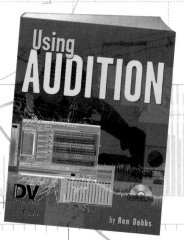

Using Audition

Ron Dabbs

Finish your video projects with compelling audio tracks. Practical examples and tutorials show you how to edit, mix, record sound, reduce noise, use loops and effects to create tracks, and apply shortcuts and workflow-integration techniques to speed production. The companion CD contains tutorial media and plug-ins.

$44.95, Trade Paper with CD-ROM, 352 pp, ISBN 1-57820-240-X

What's on the DVD

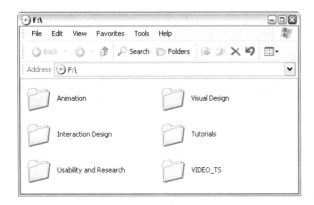

The DVD contains the following folders.

- *Animation* This has templates for creating storyboards.
- *Visual Design* This has Photoshop CS actions, an FBI warning screen, and a text file for copying and pasting special characters.
- *Interaction Design* This contains templates for creating wireframes and flowcharts.
- *Tutorials* The tutorials for chapters 7–9 are in this folder.
- *Usability and Research* This contains files that can help you plan and conduct usability studies.
- *Video_TS* This is the portion of the disc that is readable by a DVD player.

UPDATES

Want to receive e-mail news updates for Adobe Encore DVD? Send a blank e-mail to dvdmenus@news.cmpbooks.com. We will do our best to keep you informed of software updates and enhancements, new tips, and other related resources. Further, if you would like to contribute to the effort by reporting any errors, or by posting your own tips, please contact the author at dvdmenus@skidgel.com.